Mexico
28 Destinations for Leisure and Pleasure

Photos: Regula and Christian Heeb

Text: Susanne Asal · Herdis Lüke

BUCHER

Content

1 Mayan city of Palenque.
2 Pure luxury in the Hacienda Xcanatun in Yucatan.
3 Swimming in hibiscus blooms: pool in the Hotel Casa Natalia in San José del Cabo.
4 Jujumbo shrimps in vanilla sauce: exotic dishes spoil the palate in the Hotel Misión del Sol in Cuernavaca.
5 Exclusive and chic: the El Tamarindo Golf Resort on the Pacific.
6 Harvesting agaves near Tequila in Jalisco.
7 Wall paintings in Bonamak in Chiapas.
8 Colonial charm in San Cristóbal de las Casas.
9 The art of relaxation as practiced in the El Tamarindo Golf Resort.
10 Indian girl in Zinacanán in Chiapas.
11 Iguana in Campeche.

The Baja California is home to a wealth of fascinating contrasts between deserts, vast cactus forests and palm oases – such as this one at Arroyo Mulegé. The river of the same name flows on into the Gulf of California by the town of Mulegé. Founded in 1705 by Jesuits as the Mission of Santa Rosalia de Mulegé, the town has managed to keep its Mexican charm despite the growth in tourism. The area is of special interest to nature lovers. A walk through the canyon alongside the river promises sightings of many exotic birds – not to mention the unique atmosphere and stunning panorama.

Welcome to Mexico
A Journey that Satisfies All Five Senses

What is so fascinating about Mexico? Landscapes where the air is clear, as Mexican literature once put it, the impressive and mysterious Indian temples and pyramids, the abundance of flowers, the splendid colors, and nature's sheer luxuriance? The superb baroque churches, the exuberant colors of local handicrafts, the age-old Mayan rituals and Aztec dances, the festivities for the deceased on the Day of the Dead that we find so strange and yet so comprehensible?

Our hearts skip a beat as we enter huge places of worship such as Chichén Itzá or the Aztec temple of Teotihuacán, overwhelmed to see and experience such magnificent messengers from the past. The cruel, almost surreal representations of Gods from Mexico's Indian legacy on show in the museums are equally impressive. What a pleasure it is to listen to the mariachi bands on the Plaza Garibaldi in Mexico City or the joyous cascades of sound created by the marimba players in Veracruz, to watch the balloon vendors in the public parks struggle with their bunches of floating wares – or the fortune-tellers cajoling their tame birds to pick a card with a prophecy out of a tiny, carved box. The façades of so many churches and monasteries with their playful superfluity of ornaments will not let the eye rest. One thing is certain: Mexico is the sum of innumerable and varied cultural influences.

The fields of agaves and henequén in Yucatán stand in marked contrast to the dense forests in the Chiapas highlands, to the humid tropical vegetation of the tierra caliente (hot earth) in the hinterland of the Pacific Ocean, or the desert of the Baja California. Endless beaches, glittering like salt in the sun, line the inviting coastlines that sit enthroned over a great network of subterranean watercourses; volcanoes over 5,600 meters (18,400 feet) high

tower over temples in the central highlands. Peaceful ranges of low-lying hills dotted with innumerable lakes follow upon dark fields of sharp-stoned lava. The variety of beautiful natural landscapes is simply immense.

Yet there is something else that drifts over this country like a scarcely perceptible haze. Heaviness and lightness go hand in hand here. Anybody who has ever traveled through Mexico knows the skulls made of brilliantly colored icing sugar and decorated with small, sweet colored sprinkles. The Mexicans give each other these sweet skulls, labeled with the recipient's name, on the Día de los Muertos (Day of the Dead). Laughing at death is just one way of lessening the fear it inspires.

The ubiquitously popular corridos and rancheras are songs performed with machismo and dramatic leaps of melody, lamenting the unfaithful and willful wife, bemoaning departed luck that leaves only loneliness in its wake. Women's voices are raised just as powerfully – mostly to lament the unfaithful husband. No text is complete without grand passion, without the myth of steadfast yet disappointed love. The pain of life's vagaries is everywhere, and especially in the rancheras. Mexicans are at home in this world of extravagant, unfettered emotion. It is no wonder that Mexican television studios incessantly produce telenovelas that are eagerly snapped up by buyers throughout the subcontinent.

Such forms of escapism are one way of dealing with the general confusion and inscrutable corruption that characterizes daily life in Mexico. Astrid Hadad, star of theater and cabaret, once made the self-ironical comment that: "I am proud to be Mexican. It provides at least one excuse for the chaos inside me." She styles her appearance on Frida Kahlo, Mexico's most famous female artist,

whose biopic generated such excitement at the 2002 Oscar ceremony and doubtless contributed to the renewed attention that Mexico has recently enjoyed.

The beautiful and terminally sick wife of the fresco painter Diego Rivera spent her whole life dwarfed by the incessant productive stream maintained by her husband. However, in the 1970s, her semi-surrealistic autobiographical paintings won her international cult status as an icon of feminism. Chaos, joy, sorrow, tragedy and love of life are united in her personality as if she were a mirror image of her motherland. Although she was a communist, she had a weakness for expensive perfumes, loved to put on makeup and costumes, dressed in the expensively embroidered fabrics of the Zapotec women and draped coral and jade stones the size of pigeon's eggs around her neck. She admired Mexican folk art and her collection of Mexican arts and crafts contributed to the growth of their reputation worldwide. She loved Mexican cuisine and its Indian roots. The Museo Frida Kahlo in Coyoacán (Mexico City) is a must for visitors – and not only for those interested in art.

1 Exotic and exquisite: the cuisine in the Posada la Poza Hotel in Baja California.
2 Museo de Arte Moderno, Mexico City, with a painting by Frida Kahlo in the background.

Mexico is also the incomplete merging of Indian and Mestize identities. In his essay on "The Labyrinth of Solitude," the Novel Prize Literature Laureate Octavio Paz reflects on the lasting effects of the abuse and humiliation suffered by Mexicans during the Spanish conquest.

Traveling from San Cristóbal de las Casas to the Mayan communities in Chiapas, visitors will experience for themselves the rift that goes through the country. The Indian population is greatly disadvantaged when it comes to education and nutrition. But this discrepancy is not obvious because today's descendants of Mexico's indigenous population mask the shabbiness of their lives by embracing their own culture with such conviction and clarity. This is most apparent in costumes, language, and in their songs, but it is also expressed in their customs and the traditional organization of

their villages. So Mexico has a kind of dual identity – both Indian and Mestize.

This duality is most glaringly obvious during the festivities that mark the anniversary of the appearance of Our Lady of Guadalupe on December 12 – Mexico's National Day. According to legend, the Virgin of Guadalupe appeared to an already baptized Indio on Mount Tepeyac on December 12, 1567 – on the very site occupied by a temple dedicated to the mother- and earth-goddess Tonantzín. This deity, adorned with serpents and skulls, is the highest female goddess in the Aztec religion. The Virgin ordered Juan Diego to report her appearance to the church authorities, which he promptly did and with great success. The basilica built in her honor is one of Latin America's most important pilgrimage sites.

The Virgin of Guadalupe was quickly adopted by the faithful. Traces of Tonantzín were assimilated and finally absorbed in her image. Yet she is no racist Madonna or representative of the upper classes – symbolizing instead both resistance and solidarity. An image of the pale and delicate Virgin, embedded in garlands of roses and rising from a crescent moon, was carried by such revolutionary leaders as Padre Hidalgo, the "father" of Mexican independence from Spanish dominion, or by the supporters of Emiliano Zapata and Pancho Villa during the Mexican Revolution, just as it was a talisman for the Mayan rebels of the Zapatista National Liberation Army under Subcommander Marcos.

Nowadays, she also does duty as a pop icon. Along with Frida Kahlo, her image is a popular feature on linen shoulder bags embroidered with sequins. Which brings us once again to Mexico's multiformity …

The festivities in honor of the Virgin of Guadalupe on December 12 in Mexico City are another must for visitors. They take place in the Indios Verdes quarter, where the basilica is situated.

Two further religious holidays are of great significance in Mexico. On All Saints' Day and the Day of the Dead, the Mexicans visit their deceased. But not just to put fresh flowers on the grave or tidy it up for winter; they come with the fully-packed picnic hampers that we associate with summer outings, settle down, sing and light candles, staying half the night. In some communities, such as that of Sierra Norte in Oaxaca, the whole village gets together after the Day of the Dead to consume the food and drink left over by the deceased. For no one doubts that the dead are still partial to their favorite foods – even if they partake of them only in essence! The celebrations in Pátzcuaro and its eponymous lake are

1 Smart and skillful: a Mexican charro performing at a show.
2 Magic and mysticism: the flight of the voladores de Papantla from Veracruz.
3 A sweet approach to death: sugar skulls in Pátzcuaro.

numerous spectators. But they exist alongside a variety of festivals and rites that celebrate traditions more particular to Mexico itself. Whether it be the sumptuous dance festival of Guelaguetza in Oaxaca, derived from an Aztec harvest thanksgiving festival, or the costumed parades in many villages, the moros y cristianos reenactment battles that commemorate the struggle between Moors and Christians in many areas, or the voladores (bird people) in Zempoala and Papantla and their "Dance of the Flying Men."

Mexicans use these occasions to express the plurality and variety of their roots. The local calendar of celebrations is an important point of reference for villages; the regularly practiced rites constitute a cultural backbone for which every wanderer happily returns home. The festivities often take weeks to prepare and are the subject of much discussion and careful planning.

That brings us to another feature of Mexico: the big cities are attractive because they provide employment. The countryside, the village, el campo – these are the cornerstones of the individual's existence. But not everybody is able to find employment locally and agricultural production is not generally sufficient to sustain a whole family. Rural flight has taken place on a large scale – especially in the central state of Zacatecas. Recent studies have shown that about half the indigenous population now lives in the metropolis – where life is organized as if at home in the village. In Mexico, as elsewhere in the world, the big cities are the hubs of advanced civilization.

As a strictly Catholic country, Mexico gave the late Pope John Paul II the most fervent reception that he received in Latin America and boasts a collection of baroque churches of breathtaking beauty. In Taxco, famous for its silver jewelry, the lavishly decorated twin towers of the Cathedral of Santa Prisca rise up into a cobalt sky; the façade of the Church of San Francisco in Acatepec is a masterwork of finely turned pilasters; not one square inch of the interior of Santa María of Tonantzintla remains undecorated: nothing that can be turned, sculpted, carved, or covered in gold, has been left untouched. Gravity itself is overcome.

especially impressive. But they can also be witnessed in the urban atmosphere of Mexico City, where children and youngsters have turned them into a kind of Halloween. The cultural arc has been spanned from the old Indian beliefs, which hold that the dead return to earth once a year, to an imitation of North American teenage rituals.

For modern Europeans, who tend to see traditions as an obstacle to participating in a modern lifestyle, such energetically conserved, age-old customs are unusual experiences taking place, as they do, in an everyday setting far removed from folkloristic showiness. The cliff divers of Acapulco provide one kind of magic for their

But who were the painters, plasterers, bricklayers, and carpenters behind these baroque buildings? They were Indian slave workers, and they often left their mark on this architecture. They mixed tropical fruits and flowers into the carvings that decorate the columns, and smuggled creatures from their own fable and lore in amongst the saints and angels. But posterity only ever knows one name to thank for all this abundance: that of the Spanish family of sculptors and architects – Churriguera. The names of the Indian workers remain unknown.

Modern life also set up camp in the major cities. Mexico was the first country of the 20th century in which revolution swept away the old, encrusted, and unjust distribution of property. Its turbulence attracted the left-wing artistic intelligentsia. Painters, architects, filmmakers, and writers traveled to Mexico: the American photographer Edward Weston came with his muse, the Italian actress Tina Modotti; the Soviet film director Sergei Eisenstein was followed by the Spaniard Luis Buñuel. Some made friends with that most enigmatic couple of Mexican artists: Frida Kahlo and Diego Rivera, who sent out such revolutionary messages in his gigantic frescoes.

It was the Mexican sculptor Juan O'Gorman, barely 25 years old, who created the two studio-homes for Kahlo and Rivera in the Avenida Altavista in San Ángel, south of the city center. They are a triumph of classical modernity in the style of Le Corbusier – clear, plain lines with brightly-colored walls. Ricardo Legorreta produced a magical combination of clear colors and cubist forms for the National University of the Arts, the Centro Nacional de las Artes, in the Avenida Churubusco/Calzada Tlalpan. The youngest example of this synthesis between Mexico and modernity is on show to guests at the Camino Real Hotel in Mexico City. Finely plastered walls, shining colors, concrete and glass – another sample of star architect Legorreta's work.

1 An Indian family in front of its house in Veracruz.
2 A glimpse of paradise: the name says it all at the Ventanas al Paraíso Hotel.
3 Sin and saintliness: the Virgin of Guadalupe watches over Adam and Eve in a ceramic tree of life.
4 The Melía Hotel in Mexico City.
5 Private pier at the Ceiba del Mar Hotel and Spa.
6 Terraces with ocean view at the Casa de los Suenos Hotel, Isla Mujeres.

However, all this variety and fascination cannot completely dispel another image: that of poverty. No government has thus far managed to diminish the gaping rifts in society – let alone abolish their origins. A tangled, power-obsessed remnant of the formerly glorious revolution, the Party of the Institutionalized Revolution (PRI), has dominated the country unchallenged since 1928, capable even of committing murder in order to maintain power. What started out in 1928 as a socially revolutionary government dedicated to Emiliano Zapata's demands for "Tierra y libertad" (land and freedom) and that actually managed to enact some socially progressive policies in the 1930s and 40s, ended up as a corrupt "chamber of horrors." It was only in the year 2000, with the victory of the conservative PAN party under Vicente Fox, that the PRI lost power. The jovial, cowboy-like ex-Coca-Cola manager and agricultural entrepreneur Vicente Fox brought a gust of fresh air but this has long since evaporated; his policies are characterized by a lack of orientation.

Mexico has a population of just below one hundred million, the world's ninth-largest economy and seventh-largest export nation. It is a typical threshold country in which first and third worlds clash in some regions with considerable force. Despite its economic successes, Mexico comes a close second after Brazil as the Latin American country with the greatest gap between rich and poor. Ten million Mexicans are classified as rich, and one third of these belong to the super-rich who know the boutiques of Miami or Monaco better than those in Mexico City.

The middle classes, by contrast, are dwindling – whilst current unemployment figures are veiled by the shadow economy and the ingrained custom of declaring relatives as members of family enterprises.

It is not possible to streamline the experiences that Mexico holds in store. The visitor's most important asset is time. Time to travel the old-fashioned way, seeking knowledge and discovery and avoiding above all one thing – hasty judgments.

A successful journey should stimulate all five senses. That is the invitation that we extend to you as we visit 28 enticing destinations. However, there is one thing that you'll be spared: discomfort. We have suggestions for hotels and accommodation that will allow you to take a deep breath, to gather inspiration, to pause, and to reflect.

Zacatecas – the city of the silver barons.

The Heart of Mexico

Revolution and Resplendence Side by Side
The Gigantic Mosaic of Mexico City

Mexico City, the megalopolis, originally built by the Aztecs as the most magnificent and marvelous city of its time, continues to surpass all expectations. Happy the traveler who has time for a relaxed exploration of all its quarters and their oases of calm.

The fascination is greatest at night, when the illuminated city glitters luminously as far as the eye can see. Myriads of twinkling lights arise from a bed of dark velvet: Mexico City holds a splendid welcome ready for the late visitor.

Mexico City is doubtless one of the few cities upon which the term megalopolis fits like a perfectly tailored glove. An estimated population of 22 million lives under its haze, but nobody knows the exact number because some 2,000 to 3,000 workers flock here every day in search of employment. Clearly, its attractions are manifold, from the palaces described by Alexander von Humboldt, the cathedrals and the legendary Aztec temples, the huge Indian ballparks, and the baroque, gold-leaved churches. There are artists' colonies as well as bohemian dwellings, markets bursting with color and unfamiliar smells, balloon vendors in the parks, Indian quarters and Central America's answer to the Champs-Élysées, the Paseo de la Reforma.

Long ago, this city was built to dazzle all comers, whether friend or foe. It was destined to be the greatest and most magnificent city of its time. An oracle had prophesied that the great warrior nation of Aztecs would build a city on the spot where a prickly pear grew out of a stone and an eagle ate a serpent. According to historical sources, they found this spot in the year 1345 in the valley of Anahuac, at the foot of the volcanoes Popocatépetl and Iztaccíuhuatl. The Indian workers partially drained the nearby Lake Texcoco, created floating islands and built footbridges, palaces, temples, and residences for the nobility.

The Aztecs named their city Tenochtitlán and it really was a jewel. Hernán Cortés, commander of the Spanish army that conquered Mexico, wrote in 1519: "This city is so great and so beautiful that I can write only half of what there is to say about it, and even this

1 History book painted on the wall: the frescoes in the Palacio Nacional in Mexico City.
2 Toltec culture in the Museo de Antropologia.
3 That most Mexican of all cocktails, a margarita.
4 The immense dimensions of Mexico City's zócalo.

almost beggars belief, for it is more beautiful even than Grenada ... Every day there is a great market with over 30,000 buyers and sellers. All kinds of goods are on offer, from food to fabrics and garments; anything you might wish for; gold and silver jewelry, precious stones and fabulously beautiful plumage, the like of which cannot be found on any other of the world's markets ..." Naturally, this did not stop him from razing all this beauty to the ground, from destroying both the temples and the Aztec civilization.

Today, Mexico City no longer boasts the clear air that the famous writer Carlos Fuentes once praised in the title of an early novel. It has become a landscape made up of thousands of mosaic stones. Contrasting opposites exist peacefully cheek by jowl: the Aztec Templo Mayor next to Latin America's biggest cathedral, sinking slowly into its marshy foundations, the Government Palace behind the main square, the zócalo. Fortune-tellers equipped with Chinese ink sit in close proximity to that icon of modernity, the Torre Latinoamericana, and the scribes on the Plaza Santo Domingo who offer their services to the illiterate. Behind the Carrara marble that fronts the classicist temple to the arts, the Palacio de Bellas Artes, frescoes by the group of communist artists around Diego Rivera, José Clemente Orozco and David Alfaro

Siqueiros issue revolutionary proclamations: "Free yourselves from the chains of dependency, discover your greatness, your diversity and your culture," messages that one hardly expects in this spot with its golden banisters, its walls paneled with colored marble and its regular guest appearances by Plácido Domingo. Revolution and resplendence sit side by side here, shabbiness next to color, beauty next to dirty gutters, and dignity in poverty.

In 1947 Diego Rivera painted a world-famous picture of Mexico City's center: it is called "A Dream of a Sunday Afternoon in the Alameda." A plump boy smiles happily as he stands with his smartly dressed relatives next to an ostentatiously costumed skeleton in Alameda Park. The small, green lung stretches westwards from Bellas Artes down to the subway station Hidalgo under the crowns of many shade-giving trees and over well-manicured lawns on which lovers embrace and families nibble on mangos dusted with chili powder on lollipop sticks.

Let's take our first break in the pleasant cool of the Casa de los Azulejos on Avenida Madero, a branch of the chain of Sunborn restaurants that are equally popular with Mexicans and tourists alike. The beautifully tiled walls provide the perfect setting for getting acquainted with Mexican cuisine and participating in the

1 Great for family shots: the 171-meter (560 feet) high observation platform on the Torre Latinoamericana, Mexico City.
2 Street vendors spread their wares in front of the Plaza Mayor in the capital's city center.
3 Detail from a mural in the Palacio Nacional.
4 Mounted police patrol the Paseo de la Reforma. In the background: the Monumento a la Revolución.
5 Murals in the Teatro Insurgentes.

Mexican custom of having a late breakfast without automatically spewing fire like Chinese dragons afterwards. Directly opposite in the Café Opera, well-groomed waiters await customers who appreciate both the lovely vintage wood furniture – a mixture of cozy Viennese coffee house and French bistro – as well as the best margaritas in the city center. Nobody else puts together white tequila, limejuice and a dash of triple sec as well as they do here. From here, all roads lead to the zócalo: the traffic throbs, people hurry past the old-fashioned shop façades, street vendors play illegally-copied CDs at full volume and advertise their collection of Taiwanese ties. The zócalo demands to be admired: so much space, so much emptiness, and so much greatness! The classicist government building takes up a whole side of the square whilst the imposing cathedral (built from 1573–1813) slowly sinks into its

1 and 7 The Anthropological Museum in Mexico City, one of the best and biggest in the world, has the added attraction of marvelous architecture – the Golfo de México Hall is one example.
2 Double grave from the northern and eastern Mexican civilizations.
3 The stone Chaac-Mool statue in the Toltec Hall holds a sacrificial dish in its hands.
4 Female clay statue.
5 Jade mask.
6 Detail from the Quetzalcoatl temple in Teotihuacán.

swampy underground on our left. There is nothing as yet on the empty space itself except a flagpole for the national flag. Have a coffee or a cocktail on the terraces of one of the big hotels – Majestic, Holiday Inn, Gran Hotel – and settle down for some people-watching.

Let's get an overview of the area: the Aztec Templo Mayor is situated to the northwest of the cathedral. The Spanish conquerors razed the holy places of the Indians when they arrived – and the same fate befell the temple. Parts of the holy site were discovered when electrical work was being carried out on the subway station Bellas Artes. They were uncovered and the temple itself recon-structed in 1978. It is now an impressive building adorned with a number of astonishing sculptures of Indian deities, thus uniting all the centers of power – Aztec, Catholic, and secular – in the area around the zócalo.

From the zócalo, we take the bus up the Paseo de la Reforma to the Museo Nacional de Antropología — definitely the most impressive and most praised exhibition of artifacts from the Indian world in Latin America. The 65-ton statue of the rain-god Tláloc welcomes us at the entrance. The museum's treasures are spread out over 12 rooms: burial gifts from Mayan graves, including a valuable jade mask that belonged the Mayan nobleman Pakal of Palenque, stucco decorations from the pyramid of Tenochtitlán, the famous calendar stones, awesome sculptures of Aztec deities, representations of priests and wonderful jewelry. Only one thing is missing: the copilli of Moctezuma, the last Mayan ruler. This crown, adorned with the blue-green feathers of the tropical quetzal bird, is now on show in the Viennese Museum of Ethnology: stolen — say the Mexicans; legally acquired — say the Viennese.

On the first floor, the museum has attempted a scenic display of contemporary Indian ways of life, based upon the geographical classification of artworks exhibited on the ground floor — showing traditional costumes, arts and crafts, village architecture, and numerous musical instruments.

Mexico City's reputation as a city in which life is not easy is justified by the conditions that shape life in the capital. Too chaotic, too hectic, too strenuous, too much pollution, in short: a complete lack of order. Those looking for a kind of mini-Bohemia in old Mexico will find the object of their dreams in the southern suburb of Coyoacán. In the Café Parnaso, for example, where the Colombian writer and Nobel Prize winner Gabriel García Márquez likes to drink a cappuccino. The bookstore attached to the café has coffee-table books, treatises on the Zapatista National Liberation Army and Subcommander Marcos, some psychoanalysis and theater literature: a picture-book spot for intellectuals. No wonder "Gabo" feels at home here.

Let's take a seat on those strange little wire chairs around the Café Parnaso's wobbly tables. Maybe we'll get a glimpse of the lovely Vanessa Bauche, who played the role of Susana in the Mexican film Amores Perros so wonderfully. We might see the theater director Jesusa Rodríguez? Or will we espy the photographer Gabriel Figueroa, son of the famous Mexican cameraman who worked with Luis Buñuel and Sergei Eisenstein?

The heart of Coyoacán itself beats in the Café Parnaso and under the becalming shade of the cypress trees on Plaza Hidalgo. Framed on one side by the convent church of San Juan Bautista and the palace built by Mexico's conqueror, Hernán Cortés, the square is an informal marketplace for women selling gladioli and tortillas; candy floss and balloons and embroidered velvet bags are also on offer. Organ-grinders and fortune-tellers ply their trades, come rain or shine. Behind the brightly painted doors along cobblestoned alleys, houses that are home to writers, philosophers, and photographers stand side by side with theaters, antique dealers, music clubs, galleries, and museums. The Casa de Alvarado, formerly home to Octavio Paz, Nobel Prize Laureate for Literature, regularly stages exhibitions. The house in which Leo Trotsky lived during his Mexican exile is also open to the public.

The showpiece of the colonial quarter shines as brightly as lapis lazuli: the unconventional home of the famous Mexican painter Frida Kahlo (1907 – 1957), whose paintings, with their provocative subjects and apparently naïve style, seem to have sprung directly from the dreams of the Surrealists. The house reflects the artist's

1 Mexico City's great boulevard: the Paseo de la Reforma.
2 Good food in beautiful surroundings in the Casa de los Azulejos, a centrally located Sunborn-branch.
3 The glass cupola of the Gran Hotel de la Ciudad still shines as brightly as it did in the Belle Époque.
4 A golden angel watches over the city: the Independence Monument on the Paseo de la Reforma.

own love of native art, of Mexico's Indian past, of communism and of food: her kitchen, and its playfully colorful furnishings are nothing less than an invitation to sit down and feel comfortable. Some of her paintings and sketches are also on show – as well as the specially constructed bed that enabled the severely ill artist to work lying down.

Did Frida Kahlo ever go shopping, dressed – as she always was – in Mexican costume, lured by the smells of the market three streets away? Did she buy chocolate sauces, sesame, herbs and chili here for the Mexican dishes that she loved? It's well worth having a bite here, if you have the time.

On the weekend, those that can try to get out of the city. The upper classes go to their holiday homes in Cuernavaca,

Tequesquitengo or Tepoztlán; others head for some fun on the city's outskirts. One such destination is the swimming gardens of Xochimilco to the south. They are a remnant of the lagoon that originally surrounded Tenochtitlán. In former times, the farmers would anchor the floating wicker rafts, the chinampas, to the soft floor of the lagoon and plant them up with vegetables, fruit and flowers. These traditions are carried on today. The flower ladies still come here from the city to buy their wares in Xochimilco.

Xochimilco is a favorite for Sunday day-trippers. Boats decorated with flower garlands jostle for space on the water canals. Once on the water, the feasting begins. If they run out of pork rolls, visitors can stock up with the boat traders: filled tortillas, beer, tacos, and sweet, sugarcoated rolls. Music is also available: the mariachis have taken out a boat themselves and are happy to provide a gusty rendition of "Guadalajara" on demand.

Parque Chapultepec, the Park on the Locust Hill, also has a lot to offer: rowing on two lakes, long walks through the cedar woods and a visit to the castle in which the Austrian Kaiser Maximilian once resided.

Various museums surround the park, not least among them the Anthropological Museum. And because it is just so lovely here, sev-

1 The Gran Melia Hotel in Mexico City references monumental Aztec architecture.
2 An elegant suite in the Four Seasons Punta Mita Hotel in Puerto Vallarta.
3 The individually designed entrance hall of the Four Seasons Punta Mita Hotel.
4 An idyllic oasis of tranquility in the middle of Mexico City: the green, colonial-style patio in the Hotel Cortés.
5 In the Gran Melia Hotel in Mexico City.

eral hundred thousand visitors sometimes flock to Parque Chapultepec on the weekend.

Mexico City is incredibly varied. So it's a good idea to stay somewhere in the middle of the city. Many guests appreciate the pretty, secluded, and intimate Hotel de Cortés on Avenida Hidalgo. It is within walking distance to Bellas Artes, the zócalo, the cathedral, and the Templo Mayor. The former monastery dates back to 1660 and has a beautifully planted, period colonial patio.

Mexico's most famous boulevard, the Paseo de la Reforma, is home to the truly luxurious and spacious Hotel Four Seasons. Classicist design – with numerous references to old European architecture enlivened with Mexican floral motive – conveys an atmosphere of old-school European grandeur.

Mexico City – the gigantic mosaic

Getting there and when to travel
Air: the international airport Benito Juárez is situated more or less in the city center. It is advisable to purchase a fixed-tariff taxi ticket for the city transfer. These are available at specially designated counters. The airport subway station is called Terminal Aérea and is best used during the daytime and only with small items of luggage: several train changes are necessary.
Bus: leaves from the airport to Toluca, Querétano, Cuernavaca, and Puebla. Bus terminal is in front of Hall D. There are tourist information counters in Halls A and E. Four terminals: Tapo (eastwards), Observatorio (westwards), Cien Metros (northwards) and Texqueña (southwards).
Best travel time: all year round, rainy season between May and September.

Where to stay
****Four Seasons*, Paseo de la Reforma 500, Col. Juárez. Tel: 55/52 30 18 18, fax: 52 30 18 08, www.fourseasons.com
****Hotel de Cortés*, Av. Hidalgo, Col. Centro. Tel: 55/55 18 21 81, fax: 55 12 18 63, www.bestwestern.com

****Camino Real*, Mariano Escobedo 700, Col. Nuevo Anzures. Tel: 55 63 88 88, fax: 52 50 88 97, www.caminoreal. com/mexico. This huge hotel, designed by the star architect Legorreta in 1968, is a symbol of modern Mexico.

Must see
The tourist bus covers 34 km (21 miles) and 25 fixed stops that include the historical center, Polanco, Chapultepec and Plaza de las Tres Culturas; 130 museums, monuments, galleries, and parks can be visited en route.

Local attractions
One of the country's largest archeological sites is situated just north of the city. *Teotihuacán* once had a population of 200,000, making it the largest city in the world between 350 and 650 AD: the Aztecs found the deserted city in the 14th century and no one knows, even today, who the original settlers were. A magnificent avenue connects the moon pyramid to the fortress-like citadel in the southeast of the old city. But the greatest architectural feat, bigger even than the Egyptian Cheops Pyramid, is the Sun Pyramid with its five terraces, a base width of 225 meters (740 feet) and a staggering 65 meters (213 feet) height.

Information
The tourist office has a very informative website: www.mexicocity.gob.mx

Colorful, Cheerful, Inspirational
San Miguel de Allende – Mexico's City of Art

Art lovers cannot bypass San Miguel de Allende. The picturesque town with its colonial charm is regarded as the Barbizon of Mexico. Countless international artists have come to San Miguel de Allende in search of inspiration – and found it.

It's a treat just to arrive at San Miguel de Allende. Neat little houses nestle on the slopes. Swathes of bougainvillea swirl over walls and gardens. Narrow, cobblestoned alleys lead straight to the Jardín Plaza Allende, watched over by the gothic spires of the parish church of San Miguel. Innumerable galleries and boutiques selling arts and crafts products line the streets. Languages from all corners of the earth babble in the street cafés and restaurants. The façades gleam in white, light blue, pink, and beige.

San Miguel's fame as a center of artistic brilliance must be attributed to the American painter and engraver Stirling Dickinson, who came as a tourist in the 1930s. He was so taken with the little town that he settled here. In 1950, he cofounded the now famous Instituto Allende, and remained its director until 1987. The splendid building, with its gardens and the inner courtyard lined with arcades, dates back to the colonial era and is home to an art school and a language school as well as two galleries.

The town itself was founded in the 16th century as a mission, and derives its present name from the independence fighter Ignacio Allende (1779–1811), who fought alongside Father Miguel Hidalgo from neighboring Dolores Hidalgo. Situated on Mexico's silver route on the way to Mexico City, it proved a popular place to settle for mine owners from Guanajuato, Zacatecas, and San Luis Potosí during the colonial era – not least because of the pleasant climate that prevails here all year round and the thermal baths in the vicinity that were on hand to cure various ailments. The magnificent and elegant mansions that they built continue to bespeak their wealth.

Only the parish church of San Miguel seems misplaced. It was built from 1880 to 1900 on the spot where an older Franciscan church

1 The lovingly restored façades make San Miguel de Allende so endearing.
2 A flower-seller waiting for custom.
3 Just as typically Mexican as the atmosphere: the food in the Casa de Sierra Nevada.
4 The town's heart beats here on the zócalo.

1 Strange mixture of styles in San Miguel de Allende: the neo-gothic spires of the parish church.
2 Obligatory stop at the viewing point Mirador on the approach to San Miguel de Allende.
3 Alley in San Miguel Allende – travel through time to a colonial past.
4 Los Gavitanes: mariachis in search of customers.
5 Flower-seller on the Plaza Daratillo in Guanajuato.

once stood. Legend has it that the Indian master builder Zeferino Gutiérrez was inspired by a French cathedral that he had seen only on a postcard. Since its construction, the red sandstone building with its almost grotesque gothic spires has become the city symbol, visible from far away. No one should pass up the opportunity to visit the church's chapel and the statue of the Señor de la Conquista (Lord of the Conquest). Indian artisans made the figure in the 16th century using a traditional technique: separately preformed parts were glued together with a paste made from orchid bulbs and subsequently coated with lime.

The Indian master builder also constructed the church that belongs to the former monastery of La Concepción with its 12-sided dome. Today, the Centro Cultural Ignacio Ramírez is located here in this building of unsurpassed and inspirational beauty. The

cultural center is a branch of the National Institute of Fine Arts (Instituto Nacional de Bellas Artes). The adjoining café is a meeting place for teachers and pupils, who gather here to discuss and palaver over all manner of topics. The shady courtyard of the Santa

Ana public library is another ideal spot for travelers to converse with local artists. And for all those who speak no Spanish it is worth remembering that this library has the country's largest selection of English-language books.

Despite the hordes of immigrants, San Miguel de Allende has managed to retain its colonial charm – not least because the entire town is a protected monument. There are countless quaint corners, which are worth visiting. But it is above all the very special bohemian flair that makes San Miguel so attractive. Life here is quietly cheerful. No one rushes through the alleyways. Foreigners here wear folklore-style Mexican clothes to show that they "belong." They gather in small groups to chat and greet each other across the streets with a happy "Hola."

A favorite breakfast spot is the traditional café El Correo on the Jardín Plaza Allende. Our tip: try the deep-fried apple slices dipped either in cinnamon and sugar or honey. Delicious! You'll find out everything you need to know about the town here.

Let the day draw to a close in the El Agave Azul club or the Tio Lucas bar in the Angela Peralta theater, situated exactly opposite. Both these locations consider themselves the "capital del jazz sanmiguelense." Younger partygoers prefer to hang out until the early hours at Pancho & Lefty's disco with generous servings of Cuba libre and dangerously high sound levels. Many a romantic hotel is tucked away behind thick walls. Check into one of these and you'll

get a taste of what life must have been like for the town's silver barons. The only thing that's missing here is a "mozo," who traditionally serves you breakfast in bed.

Querétaro, the capital of the eponymous state, is less than one hour's drive away from San Miguel de Allende. The city's palaces, churches and monasteries, its picturesque squares, and the remains of a huge aqueduct from the colonial era make this city, founded in 1531, one of the most beautiful in the heart of Mexico. The historic conglomerate of buildings has been declared a UNESCO World Heritage Site. Querétaro is considered the cradle of Mexican independence. It was in this town that Father Miguel Hidalgo began to organize the insurgence against the Spanish colonial masters in the year 1810. The mayor's wife, the "Corregidora," supported the movement and made sure that Miguel Hidalgo was warned when danger was afoot and their plans were on the point of being exposed. Every year, this episode is reenacted in the historic setting provided by the Plaza de Armas as part of the independence celebrations in September. Emperor Maximilian of Hapsburg was executed by a firing squad in Querétaro in 1867. A chapel built on the Cerro de la Campana serves to remind visitors of this unhappy event.

San Miguel de Allende – city of art

How to get there and when to travel

Bus or car: 280 km (174 miles) from Mexico City on the Mex 57 highway in the direction of San Luis Potosí. Shortly after passing through Querétaro, a road branches off to San Miguel de Allende. Alternatively, when coming from Guanajuato, take a local road for an 85-km (53 miles) trip via Dolores Hidalgo.

Best travel time: all year round. In early summer, fields of Mexican marigolds glow in yellow and orange. The Jacaranda trees flower from January to March.

Where to stay

*****Casa de Sierra Nevada Quinta Real*. A lovingly restored colonial jewel with seven rooms in different categories (standard, luxury, suites). They are tastefully furnished and decorated with paintings by Mexican and Spanish artists. Beautiful garden with pool. The hotel is situated close to the town center. The Los Pájaros restaurant is famous for its exquisite cuisine. Hospicio 35. Tel: 415/152 70 40, fax: 152 14 36, e-mail: mail@casadesierranevada.com

Must see

International guitar festival (July), chamber music festival (August), jazz festival (November)

Local attractions

El Escondido Place: thermal baths with nine interconnected pools, some of which are covered. The pools get successively warmer. Open from 8 –18.

Cañada de la Virgen: archeological site with an 18-meter-high (60 feet) pyramid.

Atotonilco: place of pilgrimage since colonial times. The Santuario de Jesús Nazareno church with its six chapels has interesting frescoes on the walls and ceilings. It is said that Father Miguel Hidalgo stopped here on his famous independence march, took the image of the Virgin of Guadalupe from the altar and attached it to his banner, after which the Virgin was both patron saint of Mexico and patron of Mexican independence.

Dolores Hidalgo: considered the cradle of Mexican independence. On September 15, 1810, Miguel Hidalgo commanded his parish constituents to fight for independence from the Spanish, closing his speech with the words: "Viva México." This moment has gone down in Mexican history as the "Grito de Dolores."

Information

www.sanmiguelguide.com

1 Colonial past and modern service in the Hotel Casa de Sierra Nevada in San Miguel de Allende.
2 The Guacamoya suite.
3 Breakfast in the courtyard.
4 Between colonial tradition and modernity: the dining room of the restaurant.
5 Exquisite dining in historic surroundings.
6 The waiter serves vegetables and fruit from the hotel's own garden.

Relaxing in Colonial Surroundings
Cuernavaca – City of Spring

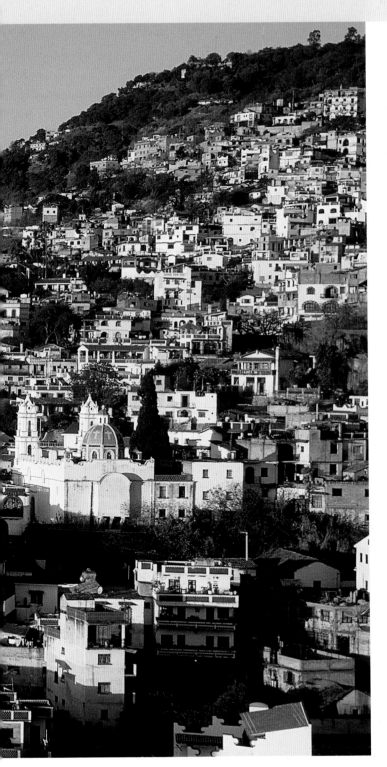

Cuernavaca is the "City of Eternal Spring." Attracted by the bounteous nature and the perennially warm climate, wealthy city dwellers from the capital have built themselves sumptuous residences here. The colonial city center is an alluring mixture of modern urban life, Bohemian world, and Indian markets

When Moctezuma, the last Aztec emperor, visited this city, it was still called Cuauhnáhuac; its name changed when the Spanish conquerors arrived under Hernán Cortés. Cuernavaca might be described as the capital city's summer garden. Located about 80 kilometers (50 miles) to the southeast of Mexico City, the "City of Eternal Spring" was once home to the summer palace of Moctezuma's mother. Cortés had magnificent rooms erected on the ruins of a pyramid, and the Hapsburg Emperor Maximilian, who reigned in Mexico briefly from 1863–1867, came to Cuernavaca for trysts with his lover.

Thanks to Mexico's most expensive highway, the Autopista del Sol with its breathtaking tunnels and bridges, it has been possible for some time now to cover the distance from Mexico City to Acapulco in about three and a half hours. It takes only about an hour to reach Cuernavaca, which lies on the way. But spring-like air quality is no longer guaranteed in the "City of Spring." The town has become industrialized. These days, a population of at least 600,000 inhabits this former idyll. Nonetheless, everybody who is anybody still makes a point of maintaining a weekend house in Cuernavaca. Flower-decked walls provide great photo opportunities. Behind them stretch the vast gardens of manorial estates.

Cuernavaca is the ideal place to relax in for a few days – just as the Aztecs once did when they came to cleanse themselves in the local baths. And it is all very easy to arrange. The Spa Hotel Mision del Sol, run by a German manageress, Renate von Dorrer, is situated in a large park just outside the city in Colonia Parres. There are no superfluous ornaments here to disturb the peace and quiet; the hotel design is almost monastic in its simplicity. Only natural materials such as clay tiles, wood, and the volcanic trachyte stone were used in construction. The rooms were designed along feng

1 Street scene in the old silver city Taxco.
2 Relaxing in some soft steam is traditional in Cuernavaca. These are the temazcalli baths in the Spa Hotel Mision del Sol.
3 Hernán Cortés, conqueror of the Aztecs, lived in this palace.
4 The twin spires of the Santa Prisca Church have always attracted attention.

1 Monastic simplicity, purist luxury: The Hotel Mision del Sol, Resort and Spa, in Cuernavaca.
2 A villa in the Hotel Mision del So.
3 Houses in Taxco, picturesquely arranged in tiers.
4 The Churrigueresque style of ornamentation on the façade of Santa Prisca Church.

shui guidelines. Lighting is indirect. Far Eastern influences and eso-
teric principles also dominate the activities and courses available at
the hotel. The menu is vegetarian: ingredients are homegrown in
the hotel garden.

After a suitable period of regeneration, it's a good idea to take a
walk through Cuernavaca's city center. The municipal authorities
have known for many years what the city's inhabitants and visitors
want: a beautifully preserved colonial city center. Which is why the
Governor's Palace also presents itself in this style, although it was
built as recently as 1967. The palace built by Hernán Cortés is situated on the east side of the zócalo – although Cortés himself took
on the title of Count of Cuernavaca only after he lost favor with
the Spanish King. Today, the palace houses the Museo de
Cuauhnáhuac and exhibits what Cortés destroyed: the remains of
an Aztec pyramid. It is worth taking time to look at the frescoes
painted by Diego Rivera in the palace loggia. They read like a banner with scenes from the revolution that center on the two free-

Cuernavaca – city of spring

Getting there and when to travel
Bus: from Mexico City Airport direct to Cuernavaca or from the Terminal del Sur at the Taxqueña subway station. The trip takes roughly one hour and ends at the bus terminal in the Calle Morelos.
Best travel time: all year round, rainy season between May and September.

Where to stay
*****Spa Mision del Sol*, Av. Gral. Diego Diaz Gonzáley 31, Col. Parres. Tel: 777/321 09 99, fax: 321 11 95, www.mision-delsol.com, Purism at its most luxurious.
*****Hosteria Las Quintas*, Blvd. Diaz Ordaz 9, Col. Cantarranas. Tel: 777/362 39 49, fax: 362 39 40, www.spalasquintas.com
Ecological walking tours, botanical gardens, Mexican diet cuisine all guarantee a pleasant stay.

****Posada del Tepozteco*, Paraiso 3, Tepoztlán. Tel: 395 00 10, fax: 395 03 23, www.mexicoglobal.com.tepozteco. Small, cozy hotel idyll with a very good restaurant.

Must see
The Museo de Cuauhnáhuac in the palace built by Hernán Cortés exhibits archeological objects found in the region. Original frescoes dating from the 17th century can be seen in the Catedral de la Asunción de María. Mariachi masses are celebrated here on Saturdays. The residence of artist Robert Brady, the Museo Brady, Calle Netzahuálcoyotl 4.

Local attractions
The silver-mining boom that began in Taxco (Tlachco), 100 km (62 miles) to the south of Cuernavaca, in the 18th century continues to this day – if the hustle and bustle in the numerous silver stores is anything to go by. The pretty colonial town that nestles in the El-Atache Mountains is watched over by the twin spires of the Santa Prisca Church, built in the Churriguera style.
The charming weekend getaway Tepoztlán offers many capital city dwellers a safe haven of peace and relaxation in bracing mountain air. It is situated about 30 km (19 miles) east of Cuernavaca.

Information
Subsecretaria de Turismo Morelos, Av. Morelos Sur No. 187, Col. Las Palmas, Cuernavaca, Morelos. Tel: 01-777/314 38 72 and 314 39 20. www.turismo-morelos@sienet.com.mx

dom fighters José María Morelos from Veracruz and Emiliano Zapata, who was born in this area. A walk up the Calle Hidalgo takes visitors to the Catedral de la Asunción de María, built in 1533 by the conquistadors on the remains of brutally razed Aztec architecture. The 17th-century frescoes, discovered by chance during renovation work and showing missionary monks at work in Asia, are the cathedral's most valuable treasure.

It is only a stone's throw to the Jardín Borda, a spacious park that easily serves as a good substitute for botanical gardens: the plants that thrive here by dappled pools and springs come from all over the world. José de la Borda donated these grounds to the city in 1763 and the Austrian Emperor Maximilian used them as a backdrop for his festivities.

The Museo Brady, home of artist Robert Brady, welcomes visitors with an enticing mixture of folk art, old monastic architecture, and convivial Mexican home décor; the North American painter had the Casa de la Torre, formerly part of a Franciscan monastery, transformed into a labyrinth of beautiful rooms.

Make sure that your itinerary includes a visit to the zócalo and neighboring Parque Juárez. In the evenings, the restaurants and cafés are filled with foreign language students polishing up their Spanish.

Butterfly Nets in the Morning Light
Michoacán and Lake Pátzcuaro

The many and varied landscapes in Michoacán make it one of the most beautiful of Mexico's states. Great store is set by tradition in the picturesque towns and villages – whether pre-Spanish or colonial.

If it hadn't been for Adriana Reyes, we wouldn't have taken the time to visit Michoacán. The state is characterized not by spectacular sights, but by varied landscapes and small colonial towns. Shimmering lakes and delicately colored meadows of flowers contrast with the fine contours of farming land, with cornfields and cattle pastures. The volcanic earth makes for fertile soil.

The pleasant little town of Michoacán is more of an insider tip than a mainstream tourist attraction. For Adriana Reyes, it is special because it boasts two things that no other Mexican state can offer: the pescado blanco and the birth of a volcano just over 60 years ago. Adriana comes from Pátzcuaro, a town situated about three kilometers (2 miles) from the lake of the same name. She works in Mexico City as an editor and is often overcome with yearning for her hometown. She misses the lyricism of butterfly nets in the morning light which the fishermen use to catch the white fish in Lake Pátzcuaro – as well as the taste of the fish itself: a very special taste, according to Adriana. And she tells us about Paricutín, the volcano whose birth was so inimitably described in 1943 by the father of all journalists, Prague-born Egon Erwin Kisch.

"In the afternoon, I see stones flying out of the crater. On their way out, they disentangle themselves from the smoke columns and bounce off in all directions. Once evening falls, however, they turn into blocks of fire that zoom towards Orion in the night sky and seem, for one brief instant, to join the stars. Once this fleeting moment has passed, they fall like flashing comets onto the mountainside …

It's as if the mountain cone were divided exactly into 360 degrees and a separate stream for each segment flowed golden from apex to base, three hundred and sixty avalanches of liquid gold."

Liquid gold avalanches and the taste of pescado blanco was incentive enough to get us climbing up the small hill that rises steeply

1 El Santuario in Pátzcuaro.
2 The All Souls' celebrations look back over a long tradition in Michoacán, here, for example, in the cemetery of Tzintzuntan.
3 Holy figurines made by Juan Torres from Capula.
4 Social event: visiting the dead on the Dia de los Muertos in the cemetery at Capula.

on Janitzio Island, in the middle of Lake Pátzcuaro. Waiters from the local restaurants praise the white fish lying on the grill as the best in the area. According to the waiters, the fish are so fresh that they were still thrashing about in the nets that very morning. Some of the outdoor restaurants have turned their stairways into terraces. You can sit down just about anywhere and enjoy this local specialty. Any building that has not been turned into a hot-food stall or a restaurant does duty as a souvenir shop – or so it appears at first view.

A monumental statue of the freedom fighter José María Morelos looks over the island from its highest point. Inside stairs take visitors up to the statue's head, where the intrepid climber can step out and view the lake and its surroundings. Evenings are the most romantic time, when thousand of candles illuminate the island and the many steps and stairs are decorated with tea lights.

Adriana tells us that the people of Pátzcuaro and the surrounding villages used to live mainly off the land: they grew corn, beans, squash, and kept cattle. Michoacán itself ("the place of the fishermen," according to the Aztec Náhuatl language) is the homeland of the Tarascans, also called Purépecha by some. They are simple

people – so they say – and were never vanquished by the powerful Aztec warlords of the central highlands, although they were ultimately unable to withstand the armies of Hernán Cortés. They themselves had no higher culture of note – such as that developed by the Aztecs or the Maya. They built neither temples nor palaces. Instead, they manufactured expressive ceramic and clay sculptures in a lively, realistic, and elegantly proportioned style that feels almost modern. Both Diego Rivera and Rufino Tamayo were enthusiastic collectors of these small stone sculptures.

It is unfortunate that these pieces cannot be viewed in Pátzcuaro itself. They are now on show in the Anthropological Museum in Mexico City and in Rufino Tamayo's museum in Oaxaca. Nonetheless, Adriana Reyes recommends a visit to the house with eleven patios, the "Casa de los Once Patios," situated in the former monastery southeast of the Plaza de Quiroga. Each of the eleven patios houses a studio manufacturing local arts and crafts: in a process that involves great precision, trays, bowls, and hollow pumpkins are covered with a coat of shiny varnish, on which myriads of colorful blooms and little birds or delicate geometric patterns are later painted. The small local Museo de Arte Popular,

1 Flower wake on the day after All Souls'.
2 Sometimes, the dead also come to visit … decorated house altar in Santa Fe de la Laguna in Michoacán.
3 Juan Torres from Capula shows his "Catrina".
4 Lavish flower decorations in honor of the dead.
5 The cemetery of Tzurumutaru.

located in a former convent one block above the Plaza de Quiroga, exhibits some examples of this traditional artisan trade. Señor Quiroga's name crops up so frequently in Pátzcuaro that a little investigation seems appropriate: who was this gentleman? Don Vasco de Quiroga (1470–1565), born in Castilian Ávila, was the first bishop of Michoacán. It is said that the Indians affectionately called him Tata Vasco, or "old man" Vasco. Tata founded a college in which young "indigenas" were trained as priests. It is that same monastery, dedicated to St Nicholas, that now houses the Museo de Arte Popular. One of Pátzcuaro's most beautiful 16th-century squares, set in the middle of a picturesque ensemble of houses, is also named for him. A second charming plaza is dedicated to the female independence fighter Gertrudis Bocanegra. What would Tata Vasco make of the festivities on All Souls' Day for which the inhabitants of Pátzcuaro are famous? The "Day of the

1 The monumental statue honoring the freedom fighter José María Morelos crowns the Isla Janitzio on Lake Pátzcuaro.
2 Traces of colonial life remain in the leisurely town of Pátzcuaro.
3 The view from the Posada La Basilica hotel is fabulous.
4 Comfortable colonial-style interior at the Posada La Basilica hotel.

Dead," one of Mexico's most important religious holidays, has an even greater significance here than elsewhere. El Día de los Muertos starts on the preceding evening with a festive procession of canoes on the lake: islands, boats, and lakeside are bathed in a sea of light. One after the other, boats dart out from the tall reeds around the San Pedrito mole, following the moonbeams reflected on the water. Next morning, the wake for deceased children, or "angelitos," begins when the faithful visit the graves to put out the sweet bread for the dead, the "pan de muerto," that is covered with icing sugar and colored sprinkles.

A real celebration dinner is given in honor of the souls of deceased adults – in expectation of their visit during the night. Members of the deceased's family gather with picnic hampers around graves that are sumptuously decorated with flowers. The smell of incense and joss sticks envelops the participants – who are not above passing round the odd bottle of tequila. The dishes that they have brought along are those that the dead used to relish. There is nothing on the table that they would not have eaten. When the dead

come back down to earth, they deserve to eat what they enjoy. Who knows what is served in heaven? One thing is clear: the dead are silent but they like to eat – even if what they consume is only the essence, the soul of the food, and not the actual substance itself. Before we take a look at what has become of the avalanches of liquid gold, let's check out our rooms in the hotel recommended by Adriana Reyes. The Posada La Basílica has a long tradition of hospitality, going back over 60 years. The colonial house that dates from the 18th century has been cleverly converted and its owners have retained both the terra-cotta floors and the wooden galleries. The rooms are equipped with many small details. Dining by candlelight on the patio is a pleasure. Rest your eyes afterwards and enjoy the lake view from the terrace.

It is worth taking a day trip to the young volcano Paricutín, often referred to as the seventh natural wonder of the world. It provides an opportunity to see one of Mexico's many corn granaries, out of which the volcano erupted. What began as a small bubble in a cornfield belonging to farmer Dionisio Pulido grew overnight into a volcano about 10 meters (33 feet) high. The volcano was active until 1952 and had by then reached a height of more than 300 meters (980 feet). The sunken Church of San José de las Colchas, immersed up to waist level in the volcanic lava, offers a strange spectacle with its two spires pointing skywards.

Michoacán and Lake Pátzcuaro

Getting there and when to travel
Air: there are airports in Morelia and Uruapán.
Bus: frequent service from Morelia, Mexico City, Guadalajara and also from Lázaro Cárdenas on the Pacific coast.).
Best travel time: like Oaxaca, Pátzcuaro is situated in the central highlands and thus also in the temperate zone, the "tierra templada," which has only slight differences in temperature in summer and winter. It is slightly warmer and more humid during the rainy season in summer.

Where to stay
****Posada La Basílica*, Arcigna 6. Tel: 434/342 11 08, fax: 342 06 59. A comfortable hotel located in a beautifully restored colonial house. Seven of the twelve rooms have open fireplaces. Excursions and boat trips arranged upon demand.

***Mansión Iturbide*, Portal Morelos 59. Tel: 434/342 03 68, fax: 342 36 27, www.mexonline.com/iturbe.htm. A slightly cheaper and more colorful alternative in a colonial-style house with cozy rooms and a terrace overlooking the Plaza. Centrally located. Bike rental.
****Hacienda Mariposas*, situated between Pátzcuaro and Santa Clara del Cobre. Tel: 434/2 47 28. www.haciendamoriposas.com. Elegantly rustic hotel with its own stables and footpaths, surrounded by 25 ha of pinewoods and orchards.

Must see
Beautiful museums and shops selling local arts and crafts products. Excursions on the lake and its islands: Isla Janitzio is the biggest and best known of these. Isla Pacanda, Tecuen, and Yunuen celebrate the Día de los Muertes with particular intensity. Boats leave from the mole, some are roundtrips.

Local attractions
The archeological site Tzintzúntzan, the last capital city of the Tarascans, is situated on the eastern shore of Lake Pátzcuaro. The unusual round pyramids, or "yácatas," rise from a large, rectangular platform. The lake view is spectacular. Trips to the Paricutín volcano must be privately organized. The surrounding villages are famous for their arts and crafts: Santa Clara for its copper products, Parocho for guitars, Ocumicho for clay devils.

Information
www.michoacan.gob.mx for tourist information.

The Mysterious Forces of Nature
At the Monarch Butterfly Sanctuary near Zitácuaro

Every year, a breathtaking natural spectacle takes place in Michoacán when millions of monarch butterflies come here to mate at the end of October. The picturesque town of Zitácuaro is our point of departure for an excursion to the Santuario de la Mariposa Monarca.

It is early in the morning in Zitácuaro and still quite cool outside. The picturesque mining town lies in the middle of a huge biosphere reserve (56,260 ha) in Mexico's central highlands. The streets are still empty in the dawn light as we get into the jeep with our young guide and make our way to the Cerro de la Campana, more than 3,000 meters (9,800 feet) above sea level. We cover the last stretch on foot. The sun hardly penetrates the dense pines. Only occasionally do we get a glimpse of one of these beautiful orange-white-black patterned butterflies. Where are the remaining millions?

Our guide, Ignacio, called Nacho, whispers "sshhh!" — signaling the need for complete quiet and points to long, dark lumps hanging from the branches all around us. They look like the bird's nests that I once saw in the tropical rainforest of Tabasco. As if responding to Nacho's "sshhh!" the nests open. The higher the sun rises, the more nests open. As soon as a ray of sun touches a nest, it opens and swarms of butterflies fly up into the sky. Soon, the air is full of orange-black dots. It is an overwhelming sight.

It is hard to believe that this butterfly refuge was not discovered until 30-odd years ago. A Canadian butterfly specialist caused a sensation when he discovered the Monarch's winter quarters in the majestic Sierra Madre in 1976. Up to that point, Canadian and American naturalists had always noticed that the Monarchs disappeared for winter, but no one knew where they went. The Mexican farmers thought they might be a pest and used water hoses to try to get rid of the butterflies. Once they had been correctly identified, the Mexican government acted quickly and declared the entire area a natural reserve, with only a few points of entry. The Cerro de la Campana belongs to the El Rosario "ejido" — a kind of

1 Route Mex 15 from Morelia to Cuidad Hidalgo.
2 Poinsettia farm near Ciudad Hidalgo.
3 Refueling in the sun: Monarch butterflies in the biosphere reserve in Michoacán.
4 Waking up in the morning light: as soon as a sunbeam reaches their nest, the Monarch butterflies are up and away.

1 Albergue Don Bruno in Angangueo.
2 Gardens of the Albergue Don Bruno.
3 On the way to visit the Monarch butterflies.
4 Lisa and Pablo spoil their guests in the Rancho San Cayetano in Zitácuaro.
5 Room in the Rancho San Cayetano.

cooperative whose inhabitants profit from their participation. Much of their income is generated by the services that they provide.

It is now known that the Monarch uses ultraviolet light to orientate itself on its 4,000-km (2,480 miles) journey. Neurobiologists have discovered that the butterflies have special sensors. The ultraviolet light also provides the signal for their departure. They fly at a height of up to 2,500 meters (8,200 feet) and never deviate from their path. It's fascinating listening to Nacho's explanations whilst thousands of butterflies warm their wings in the sun before swarming to a trickle of water to drink – their breakfast, so to speak. The earth is transformed into a carpet made of tens of thousands of colorful butterflies – one hardly likes to move for fear of stepping on them. It's heartbreaking to see thousands of dead butterflies on the path later on. But it's not our fault: "The male dies after mating," Nacho reassures us.

Our early departure was worth the effort. During the morning, the woods fill up with tourists and noisy school classes and it becomes clear why access to the biosphere reserve is so strictly controlled. Visits are supposed to last a maximum of 90 minutes

but hardly anyone sticks to this limit. Traveling and camping within the reservation is prohibited, but this, too, is hard to control in such a large area. Some locals are happy to act as guides for "off-the-beaten-track" tours in return for a few pesos. But it is not only tourism that threatens this unique insect. Illegal deforestation and forest fires aimed at land gain, as well as climate change, are further factors endangering the Monarch butterfly. The winter of 2002 was a catastrophe: a cold front moved through the area, killing almost 90 percent of an estimated butterfly population of 37 million.

Torn between the euphoria of witnessing such an amazing natural spectacle and the bad conscience that bothers us for staying too long in the Monarch butterfly's sanctuary, we finally return to Zitácuaro. The town is proud of its heroic history. It burned to the ground three times: the first time during the War of Independence (1810), then again in April 1855 upon the order of the legendary President Santa Ana, and once more during the French intervention (1864–1867). Mexico's first independent government was founded here – no wonder, then, that the town is full of monuments.

Zitácuaro – the mysterious forces of nature

Getting there and when to travel
Air: airports of Mexico City (about 170 km/105 miles), Morelia (about 150 km/93 miles) and Toluca (about 97 km/60 miles).
Bus and car: from Mexico City on the toll highway via Toluca to Morelia.
Best travel time: October to April.

Where to stay
*****Rancho San Cayetano*. The rustic hotel is situated within an area of approx. 5 ha that includes dense forest, a gorge, and a small river. It has a beautiful garden with pool, nine double rooms. and three airy bungalows – small but comfortably appointed with a view over the gorge and the river. The hotel is part of the "Tesoros de Michoacán" (treasures of Michoacán) chain. French and Mexican cuisine. Carretera a Huetamo km. 2.3, Zitácuaro. Tel: 715/153 19 26, fax: 153 78 79, e-mail: hotel@ranchosangayetano.com, www.tesorosmichoacan.com

***Casa Don Bruno. This simple hotel in the little town of Anganguero is a meeting place for many tourists. A good place to hire local guides for individual tours of the biosphere reserve.

Must see
The Monarch Butterfly Festival (in February). The topic dominates the whole region with exhibitions, readings, lectures, workshops.

Local attractions
San Felipe de los Alzati: a village inhabited by Otomi Indians 9 km (6 miles) to the north of Zitácuaro. San Felipe Church, the Capilla de la Candelaria and archeological digs are worth visiting. An important ceremonial center for Matlazinca rites. Open from 10–17.
Tziranda grottoes: About 10 km (6 miles) down route Mex 15 from Cuidad Hidalgo. The caves, with their strange illuminated formations, are home to 19 species of bat. Fossilized leaves and roots are also interesting. This is where the independence hero Father Miguel Hidalgo hid from his persecutors.

Information
www.tesorosmichoacan.com
www.turismomichoacan.gob.mx

Mystical, Magical, Intriguing
Uruapán and the Church in the Lava

Nowhere else in Mexico is the synthesis of Indian tradition and colonial history as tangible as here in Uruapán. Only here, close to the Paricutín volcano, stuck in a barren, lava landscape is there a church whose spire points heavenward like God's own admonitory finger.

It's a little as if time had stood still here. Our own deep breaths and the snorting of our horses are all we can hear apart from the wind whistling over dark boulders of lava. We have come five strenuous kilometers (3 miles) since departing from the village of Angahuán near Uruapán. There are only a few meters left before we reach the baroque spire of San Juan Parangaricútiru that still rises solid and unscathed from the lava whilst only traces of its former twin survive. A fantastic image – but a macabre one. When the earth began to heave under the feet of the corn farmer Dionisio Pulido on the afternoon of February 20, 1943, he witnessed a natural spectacle never before seen by human eyes: the birth of a volcano. There are no records of this ever having been observed before. His eyewitness account went down in history. Every guide in Angahuán knows it by heart.

No wonder, then, that our guide Miguel also tells the story of the peasant who went to his fields in the morning and found them unusually warm, warm enough to almost burn his feet. Later in the day he watched, aghast, as the earth suddenly split open, issuing smoke and fire, and spewed up huge chunks of rocks accompanied by deafening sounds of hissing and cracking. He never made it back to his modest hut. It had already been reduced to ashes whilst his cornfield was burning brightly. Everywhere, people were fleeing from the fire and the flying rocks, the smoke and the suffocating steam. The volcanic eruption itself began around midnight. Huge blocks of lava rocketed out of the volcano as if it were a cannon. On the third day, streams of lava finally poured out of the ground, burying forever an area of 18.5 square kilometers that included flourishing fields and several villages – only the pretty church spire of the district town of San Juan Parangaricútiru remained. The local inhabitants only just managed to take down the figure of Christ from the altar before they had to flee.

1 Horse and guide waiting to take visitors to the volcano.
2 Indian women in front of the church in Angahuán.
3 Immovable in the lava: the walls of San Juan Paragaricútiru.
4 Symbiosis of agriculture and nature: Eduardo Ruiz National Park.

1 The Rio Grande de Morelia near Zinapecuaro.
2 Meeting of the waters: River Cupatitzio in the Eduardo Ruiz National Park near Uruapán.
3 The inhabitants of San Juan Parangaricútiru could save only the statue of Christ from the encroaching lava masses.

About 3,000 to 5,000 people – the exact numbers are not known – lost their homes. 4,500 cattle and 550 horses perished in this inferno. Although there were no human casualties, Miguel is still full of indignation when he tells us that: "It took the Red Cross three months to get here, in May, and help the locals!" By that time, it was just a question of settling disputes – resettling the homeless, calculating compensation and clarifying property issues. At this stage, the volcano had reached a height of 50 meters (164 feet). By October, the cone was 365 meters (1,200 feet) high.

In October 1953, nine years after its eruption, the volcano was extinct. Of course, scientific explanations abounded: this particular volcano was of the "monogenetic" type that becomes extinct fairly quickly after its eruption. But the locals have another explanation for the end to their inferno. Legend has it that the figure of the Holy Virgin of Hope (Vírgen de la Esperanza) was visiting Angahuán (patron saints are often carried to other towns and villages within the highlands of Mexico for local celebrations and processions). Three priests were celebrating Mass in a local tower and prayed to the Virgin to intercede on behalf of the suffering populace. When the inhabitants of the neighboring villages awoke next morning, they found Paricutín as quiet as a mouse: and that's the way it has stayed ever since. The volcano is 424 meters (1,390 feet) high. Its crater has a diameter of approximately 250 meters (820 feet) and a depth of roughly 35 meters (115 feet).

Going up the volcano is arduous – and not only because it is situated over 3,000 meters (9,840 feet) above sea level. The ascent should not be undertaken without a proficient guide: on foot, on a donkey or a horse. There is no point in just setting out over the lava. The guides know the way. Those without proper walking boots

or shoes with rubber soles should stick to the vista from the out-look point El Mirador in Angahuán, which affords a good view of the lava field and the pink sandstone spire. Sufficient parking is available and there is a small museum and a bar. If asked to do so, the barkeeper is happy to show a 15-minute film on the history of the volcano.

The next morning in Uruapán we were forced to admit that we should have looked at the town before going to the volcano. Nonetheless, our aching muscles did not deter us from enjoying this little urban gem.

Uruapán is located right in the middle of the realm of the Purépacha to the east of Michoacán on the banks of the River Cupatitzio, which has its source nearby in the Parque Nacional Eduardo Ruiz. The town's name derives from the Purépachan original "Ulhupani" – place of everlasting flower and growth. Abundantly verdant gardens with tropical flowers invite one to linger. Favored by a mild climate, the town is situated in a paradise

at about 1,600 meters (5,200 feet), surrounded by a wonderfully graceful landscape with wooded hills and lush pastures. The town's reputation as Mexico's "avocado capital" and orchard comes from the vast avocado and fruit plantations in the surrounding area. Founded in 1533, the town has managed to retain its colonial charm and Indian traditions despite its now considerable popula-tion of nearly half a million.

There are six districts, or "barrios," and each has its own chapel and its own character. And the barrios of San Miguel, San Pedro, San Francisco, Santa María Magdalena, San Juan Bautista, and Santo Santiago still retain their individual style and their independence. Red-tiled roofs supported by often elaborately carved pillars emphasize the town's charm.

The immaculately maintained old town is set out like a chessboard around the two-part main square, originally conceived as a market place. This is where the Franciscan friar Juan de San Miguel founded the first Indian hospital in Latin America in the very same year as

1 Mansión del Cupatitzio Hotel in Uruapán.
2 Manorial idyll: patio in the Mansión del Cupatitzio Hotel.
3 Room with a view over the magnificent gardens of the Mansión.
4 Untouched: Lake Jaripo near Emiliano Zapata.
5 Up to its spire in lava: San Juan Parangaricútiru.

the town's foundation, directly next to the Church of the Immaculate Conception.

The hospital chapel's beautifully worked portal features a statue of the "Saint of Uruapán," whom the Indians revere as "Tata (or "Papa" in Purépacha) Juanito." Today, the Museum of Folk Art is located in La Huatápera.

Michoacán is famous for the variety of its native arts and crafts. Uruapán, for example, produces trays and trunks decorated with inlay technique as well as splendid lacquer work and handwoven fabrics. The clever priest encouraged the Indians to learn a craft and they bequeathed to posterity beautiful carvings and frescoes in the churches. Knowledge and skill are passed on from generation to generation. These wonderful handicrafts – including textiles, costumes, and ceramics – can be bought in the Casa del Turista in the town center. The arts and crafts market that takes place annually on Palm Sunday is legendary, and 1,200 artisans come from all over Michoacán to join in a procession that is alphabetically ordered according to the town and village names and led through the town by their respective elders. With over one million products, the market is the biggest in Latin America.

The wealth of Purépachas cultural heritage is evident in the many festivals that take place during the year in the barrios of Uruapán and its surroundings. The magic and mystery of the area is fully expressed in the Purépacha dances and ceremonies that form a synthesis with Spanish and Moorish influences. The regional cuisine is also part of the local culture. The exhibition of gastronomical products presented by the Purépacha on Palm Sunday is famous far beyond the borders of Michoacán. And because the cuisine is so delicious and so varied there is even a separate market for delicacies, the "Mercado de Antojitos," with booth after booth smelling of herbs and exotic spices. Our recommendation: Sopa Tarasca, Pollo Placero, and Ate de Zaramora with its very special, firm blackberry jelly to finish with. The market is open until late at night.

Uruapán – mysterious, magical, intriguing

Getting there and when to travel
Air: from Mexico City to Uruapán.
Bus and car: from Mexico City via Toluca in the direction of Guadalajara (toll highway), exit for Morelia-Uruapán. Alternatively, on route Mex 15 from Toluca via Zitácuaro and Cuidad Hildalgo.
Best travel time: October to June.

Where to stay
*****Mansion del Cupatitzio on the edge of Eduardo Ruiz National Park*. Lovely hotel built in the local rustic style. Large pool in beautiful garden. 53 rooms and a suite decorated with regional artwork. Walking tours possible from the hotel through the National Park, passing by its waterfalls. The River Cupatitzio can be seen from the restaurant. Cuisine: regional and international. Specialty: Trout Tarasca. Calzada de la Rodilla del Diablo 20. Tel: 452/523 21 00, fax: 524 67 72, e-mail: reservaciones@mansiondelcupatitzio.com, www.mansiondelcupatitzio.com

Must see
Fiestas de Reyes (Epiphany) with the famous dance of the Curpites. January 7–9 in San Juan Nuevo, about 10 km (6 miles) from Uruapán. Bachelors wear their traditional costumes on their way to visit their brides. Prizes are awarded for the most beautiful costumes and dances.
Women Water Carriers' Procession (Desfile de las Aguadoras) every Palm Sunday in the center of Uruápan.
Fiestas del Señor de los Milagros (Lord of Miracles). September 13/14. In San Juan Nuevo, a big festival takes place in honor of the statue of Christ that was saved from the Church of San Juan Parangaricútiru after the eruption of Paricutín.
The world's narrowest house. According to the Guinness Book of Records, it is 1.40 meters (4.60 feet) wide and 7.70 meters (25.30 feet) high. Carillo Puerto No. 50c, Uruapán.

Local attractions
La Tzararacua: huge waterfall in the River Cupatitzio, approx. 12 km (7 miles) to the south of Uruapán in the direction of Nueva Italia.
Paracho: about 25 km (15 miles) from Uruapán in the direction of Zamora. The town is famous for its wooden musical instruments, above all guitars, which are manufactured here in numerous workshops. The National Guitar Festival is held here in August.

Art and Tradition in Colonial Splendor
The Magical Town of Morelia

Its name is synonymous with aristocratic beauty, poetry and music – Morelia: capital of the state of Michoacán. Traditions still play a role here, such as those of wrought metalworking in the copper city Santa Clara del Cobre.

An indescribable sky of dark purple stretches over the cathedral. Its baroque spires shine imperiously under the white spotlights. It is the blue hour in Morelia, when the sun has said farewell to the day and the night has not quite arrived. This is when the town shows itself at its most dignified and splendid. After work, people meet up in cafés, young couples withdraw into the romantic parks or listen to the serenades on the zócalo.

The historic old town with its majestic palaces, former monasteries, and baroque churches is a UNESCO World Heritage Site and bedazzles with its charm. Morelia hosts numerous international festivals. Its university is considered one of Mexico's most important intellectual centers. Franciscan monks founded a mission in Morelia in 1537. A city charter was awarded four years later on behalf of the Viceroy of New Spain, Antonio de Mendoza, and the town was named Valladolid. In 1829, the city was renamed Morelia in honor of the priest and freedom hero José María Morelos, who was born here in 1765. The city owes its wealth to the rich Spanish plantation owners and to the cattle and horse ranchers in the region who built their town houses here. Morelia is situated in the heart of a fertile valley not far from Pátzcuaro on the banks of the Río Grande de Morelia.

The town's beauty, however, is not all original. The War of the Reform in the mid-19th century, which resulted in a victory of the anti-clerical liberals over the clerical conservatives, led either to a secularization of many monasteries and churches or their complete neglect. Many were only rediscovered as architecturally or historically valuable buildings in the 20th century and subsequently restored. Today, they are used mostly for cultural purposes such as museums or, as in the case of former Dominican Convent Santa Catarina de Sena, for teaching purposes. The Conservatorio de las

1 If these walls could talk: in the Government Palace of Morelia.
2 The art of the coppersmith on display in Santa Clara del Cobre.
3 Wood with a soul: carvings by Salvador Vargas in Michoacán.
4 The reflected glory of copper: shops on the zócalo of Santa Clara del Cobre.

Rosas is the oldest music conservatory on the American continent.

The economic upswing that took place during the Porfiriat (so called after the dictatorship of Prasident Porfirio Díaz, which lasted for more than three decades from 1876 to 1911) left its mark on the town's architecture. Many of the old colonial mansions were given neoclassical or art nouveau face lifts. One good example is the Palace of Justice (Palacio de Justicia). Another city symbol worth visiting is the aqueduct constructed in the late 18th century in the eastern part of the old town.

Morelia's museums are worth visiting not only for their exhibitions but also for their architectural beauty. This is true above all with regard to the regional museum, in which exhibits from the pre-Spanish and colonial era are on show in a splendid baroque building, as well as the National Museum (Museo del Estado), also known locally as the House of the Empress, or "Casa de la Emperatriz." This is where the wife of Emperor – and General – Agustín de Itúrbide, Doña Ana Huarte, spent her childhood. The cathedral on the eastern side of the charmingly arcaded zócalo is a further musical and aesthetic delight. The organ, built in Germany in 1903, is one of the largest in the world. Famous organists come here to play. The votive images are interesting and the paintings should not be missed. Michoacán's reputation as the soul of Mexico is well earned. Indian traditions are maintained here like a valuable treasure. The variety and diversity of local folk art is unmatched, as a visit to the Palacio de las Artesanías in the former monastery of San Francisco will prove. Santa Clara del Cobre is world-famous for its beaten copperwork, some of which is still manufactured with techniques dating from pre-Spanish times. Officially, the pretty town is called Villa Escalante and is located just after Pátzcuaro on the road between Morelia and Uruapán. The Bishop of Pátzcuaro, Vasco de Quiroga, had a big copper foundry erected here at the beginning of the colonial era. Production continued until the end of the 18th century before falling victim to a fire. Copperware in all shapes and sizes, often decoratively painted, is on sale in the shops: the Tarascans manufactured copper masks and rattles before the Spanish conquest. The coppersmiths are happy to let people watch them at their work – in the huge workshop of the internationally renowned artist Ana Pellicer, for example.

Morelia – art and tradition in colonial splendor

Getting there and when to travel
Air: from Mexico City or Guadalajara.
Bus and car: about 3.5 hours from or Guadalajara on toll highway.
Best travel time: October to June.

Where to stay
*****Hotel Los Juaninos*. Founded 1886 in a former bishop's palace and completely restored in 1998. Great colonial charm. 20 double rooms, 7 junior suites, and 3 master suites. Fantastic view over the zócalo and the cathedral from the La Azotea restaurant. Exquisite new Mexican cuisine, good wines. Av. Morelos Sur 39. Tel: 4 43/312 00 36, fax: 312 00 36, e-mail: juanisos@hoteljuaninos.com.mx, reservaciones@hoteljuaninos.com.mx, www.hoteljuaninos.com.mx

*****Villa Montana Hotel & Spa*. Built in a rustic-colonial style, the hotel is considered one of the best in town. 36 very comfortable, cozy rooms and suites. Pool in a wonderful garden with a breathtaking view over the town. Patzimba 201. Tel: 443/314 02 31 and 314 01 79, fax: 315 14 23, e-mail: res@villamontana.com.mx, hotel@villamontana,com.mx, www.villamontana.com.mx

Must see
International guitar festival in Morelia (March).
International Music Festival with concerts, opera, readings (November).
New Year's festival celebrated by the Purépacha Indians, held each year on February 1–2 in a different Purépacha village. The Dance of the Elderly, "Danza de los Viejitos," is fantastic.
Local attractions
Augustine Monastery Cuitzéo (30 km/19 miles from Morelia) and Yuriría (a further 35 km/22 miles) to the north of Morelia on route Mex 43 to Guanajuato.
Mil Cumbres (1,000 hills) panorama point. 70 km (43 miles) from Morelia. The road to Toluca winds its way through wonderful coniferous forests to a height of 3,100 meters (10,200 feet).

Information
Secretaria de Turismo, Nigromante No. 79. Tel: 01-800/450 23 00 (toll free), 443/312 80 81, 312 04 15, e-mail:sectur@michoacan.gob.mx, www.turismomichoacan.gob.mc, Asociación Tesoros de Michoacán, Patzimba 201-C. Tel: 01-800/503 44 09 (toll free), 443/324 81 68, e-mail: info@tesorosmichoacan.com, www.tesorosmichoacn.com

1 Church of Santa Clara del Cobre.
2 Coppersmiths in Felicitas' workshop still use Tarascan methods.
3 Colonial atmosphere in the Hotel Villa Montana in Morelia.
4 Hotel with tradition: Los Juaninos.
5 Swimming with a view: pool in the Villa Montana.

Mariachis, Fiery Riders and Tequila

Her Majesty Guadalajara Requests the Pleasure of Your Company

Nowhere else do the mariachi bands sing so wonderfully of love and heartache and nowhere else do the men dress themselves with such bravado and elegance as the "Charros" do during their riding tournaments. And it is from Jalisco that tequila started its victorious crusade around the world.

Visitors arriving from the station or the airport might suffer some initial disappointment. As with every megalopolis, the traffic lumbers through the city in the Atemayac valley under a veil of smog. But as soon as one reaches the city center, Guadalajara – capital of the state Jalisco and second-largest city in Mexico – presents herself in all her glory. Four generously laid-out squares give the cathedral a majestic framework. Traffic is banned underground whilst elegant shopping centers and wide pedestrian malls invite visitors to perambulate through the town amidst colorful flower beds, playful fountains, statues, and monuments. It's hard to believe that for centuries this city lived a life in the shadows, merely a provincial capital far from Mexico City in distance and reputation. Before colonization, this area was little more than a transit space for Indian tribes from the north who had little with which to resist the advance of the Spanish conquerors. Only industrialization in the 19th century was able to give Guadalajara the jumpstart that it needed. Guadalajara stands for the mixture of European and pre-Spanish traditions. Most of the customs and habits stem from this era. In fact, Guadalajara did not really boom until after the revolution (1910–1917).

The Hospicio Cabañas on Plaza Tapatía is a unique example of 19th-century Mexican neoclassical architecture. Completed in 1845, this splendid building with its 23 courtyards today houses the National Cultural Institute of Cabañas. Originally, it was built by the famous architect Manuel Tolsá as a poorhouse at the behest of the Bishop of Guadalajara, Juan Ruiz Cruz de la Cabañas. The east-west axis measures 164 meters (538 feet), the north-south axis measures 146 meters (480 feet). In those days, the building was

1 Mexico's national drink: tequila.
2 A typical "jimador" harvesting agaves on the fields in Sauza near Tequila.
3 Famous for its beauty: El Éden in Mismaloya has attracted bathers such as Elizabeth Taylor.
4 Mexico's charros: synonymous with manliness, sportsmanship and elegance.

the largest civilian installation in Mexico. A chapel supported by four slim columns stands in the center. It was here that the fresco painter José Clemente Orozco, a native of Guadalajara (1883–1949), painted a series of monumental wall paintings encompassing four elements: art, science, the Spanish Conquest, and the apocalypse. In 1997, UNESCO declared the Hospicio Cabañas and Orozco's frescoes a World Heritage Site. More of Orozco's wall paintings can be admired in the Government Palace (Palacio del Gobierno) on the Plaza des Armas as well as in the university auditorium. His house and studio are now a museum (Avenida Aceves 27, not far from the Triumphal Arch). In addition to sketches and paintings, the museum also has photos and letters belonging to the artist and displays some of his possessions. Liberation Square (Plaza de la Liberación) with the Degollado

Theater is also impressive. The portal rests on Corinthian columns. Frescoes depicting scenes from Dante's Divine Comedy decorate the massive dome. It is here in Guadalajara that world-famous Spanish tenor Plácido Domingo, who grew up in Mexico, began his breathtaking career.

Agua Azul, one of the city's most beautiful parks, can be reached via Calzada Independencia. On Sundays, the park is full of life as Mexican families come with old and young to picnic, play – and watch the charros. Street vendors wander around with huge bunches of brightly colored balloons. There are innumerable stands selling candyfloss in pink and light blue, as well as sweets, potato chips, and spicy corn on the cob. Brash youngsters fool around fully clothed under the fountains. The Casa de las Artesanías is well worth a visit.

Guadalajara's surroundings are famous for their clay products. The centers of production are in Tonalá and Tlaquepaque. These once used to be separate villages but have now been swallowed by the suburbs.

Music is the breath of life in Guadalajara. Guadalajara is music. Early afternoon sees the musicians making their way to and rapidly filling the Plazeula de los Mariachis between Javier Mina and Obregón. With their huge sombreros, their tight trousers decorated with silver coins, and their short jackets, they wait here for potential customers amongst the tourists or a request for a serenade, a birthday party, or a wedding. Music is everywhere, as one group tries to outplay the other. Wonderful tenor voices reverberate across the square accompanied by guitars or accordions as the mariachis sing of deception and love, of heroism and patriotism. Sometimes the

1 Patriotic: the Plaza de la Liberación with the Degollado Theater in the heart of Guadalajara.
2 Inspired by French art nouveau: the "kiosk" on the Plaza de la Liberación.
3 The Sauza family museum breathes life into the history of tequila.

songs are sweet and somber – sometimes they are cheerful and lilting, like the famous "Jarabe Tapatío." There is no better personification of the Mexican soul with its typical melancholy and its love of life than the mariachi.

No conclusive theory exists on the origins of this tradition. One school of thought maintains that it stems from the French occupation, when bands played for weddings or "mariages." But these bands were around long before the French invasion in 1864. The fact is that the mariachis are a cultural phenomenon that has

developed over a long period of time and incorporates both pre-Columbian and Spanish influences.

The same applies to the charros, the horsemen famous for their richly decorated costumes and riding skills. As far as can be ascertained, their origins lie in the Spanish colonization, since it was the Spaniards who first introduced horses to Mexico. Only the Spanish colonial masters were initially entitled to ride horses. Indians were employed only later as stable boys. The village elders and guards were subsequently also allowed to ride – bareback – in order to supervise the huge plantations. Some of these proved exceptionally talented and developed their own individual style of riding that combined dance elements with sporting excellence. The horse no longer served merely as a means of transport. Parades and tournaments were later arranged at special social events, religious or political occasions. Over time, the riders developed their own individual style of clothing that varied depending on seniority and also on the occasion. Their excessive decoration brought them close in style to the charros of Spanish Salamanca, Málaga, Toledo, and Segovia. Later, the Indians began to copy their masters and integrated a number of shapes and patterns, fabrics, colors into their

1 Agaves need eight years to ripen before they can be harvested.
2 The fruit slides down into vats to be cooked and stamped.
3 Near Tequila: blue agaves as far as the eye can see.
4 – 5 Añejo Tequila is matured in wooden vats for up to ten years before it finds its ways onto supermarket shelves.

costumes. The Aztec influence can be seen in the generous use of gold and silver brooches. The saddles, sometimes manufactured in leather from local animals, have uniquely decorated and beaten straps.

The charreriá has spread from the state of Hidalgo to the areas surrounding Mexico City, Guanajuato, San Luis Potosí, Michoacán, Guerrero, Colima, Jalisco, and Sinaloa. Today there are lienzos charros (arenas) throughout the whole country. Costumes differ according to the region and the occasion. A gala uniform can cost up to several thousand dollars. Ladies' costumes also show variations: from the colorful flounces and frills of Spain to elegant costumes in black or gray with silver embroidery and a long, narrow skirt. Status-conscious Mexicans always get married in charro uniforms, and the tournaments themselves are more than just a sporting event to showcase lassoing or cattle-roping skills. Elegance and appearances are also evaluated. Charros stand for tradition and social standing and the men are highly respected and very popular. In their smart uniforms, they are the very personification of Mexican machismo in the best possible sense: elegant, almost majestic, coquettish, handsome – and real gentlemen. When they

ask a lady to dance, they do so within the confines of a ritual that is unimaginable in Western Europe: they court the lady, dance around her, "capture" her. It is this that makes the charro games such an exceptionally sensual – and truly Mexican – experience. Their folk dances, especially the "jarabe tapatío," are a firework of rhythm, lust for life, and color. Guadalajara is the only city with its own museum dedicated to charrería art and history.

No meal, no celebration, and no evening without tequila. Mexico's national drink derives its name from the pretty town of Tequila, about 80 km (50 miles) northwest of Guadalajara. The landscape is picturesque and typically Mexican: the eponymous volcano and the Sierra Madre dominate the horizon – fields of agaves as far as the eye can see. Mexico produces approximately 190 million liters of the "drink of the Gods" each year and over half of this is exported. Over 250 different varieties are available. The Aztecs were the first to appreciate the juice of the agaves, the "maguey." The fermented pulp that forms the basis for tequila is still derived from this juice today. Without the addition of natural sugars it tastes ghastly, at least for European taste buds. But once it has been mixed with the red cactus fruit tuna it has a deliciously refreshing note. Real tequila

is made exclusively from the blue, Weber's agave. Like French champagne and cognac, the name is internationally patented. Based in Guadalajara, the National Tequila Council, or "Consejo Regulador del Tequila," consisting of local tequila producers keeps a strict eye on the quality.

The biggest tequila producer is the José Cuervo Factory in Tequila. Founded more than 200 years ago, it sets great store by tradition. The factory itself looks like a manorial hacienda. Sweet, heavy scents drift across the fields. Blue agaves need at least eight years to mature, so we are told by Sonia, who does credit to the reputation of "tapatías" as the most beautiful women in Mexico. She drives us to the fields where we meet Ismael Gama. With 35 years of experience under his belt, he is the "cuervos" – the "presentation jimador." The word "jimador" derives from "jimo" (harvest). A "jimador" is someone who tends and harvests the agaves. It is his job to regularly hack off with a machete the leaves that are too long – so skillfully that it looks as if a barber were trimming a huge beard. If the heart is ripe, the pointed leaves are cut off altogether. A good jimador such as Ismael can harvest as many as six tons per

1 Living the life of former colonial masters: Villa Ganz in Guadalajara.
2 Journey through time on the terrace of the Villa Ganz.
3 Like an oasis: the Villa Ganz's lush garden.
4 A feeling for tradition: hosts Sally Rangel and Klix Kaltenmark are passionate antique collectors.

day. Mountains of these piñas, which look like oversized pineapples, are heaped in the distillery courtyard. The fruit is cooked in giant vats, mashed, fermented with natural yeasts, and distilled at least twice in traditional column stills. The quality depends on the length of time allowed for the liquid to mature. Whilst white tequila is bottled immediately, the "Oro" and "Reposado" tequilas distilled in oak barrels need at least three months to mature and the "Añejo" tequila requires ten years to acquire its rich, brown color. Like a good cognac, it develops its soft aroma only after it has been swallowed. Protected like gold nuggets, the barrels containing the most valuable varieties lie locked up in a huge storage depot.

One Austrian distiller learnt to his cost just how powerful the Tequila Council is. In the 1990s, he put his own tequila on the market to great acclaim. Distilled three times, Don Porfidio was a particularly fine drop that even won international prizes – something hitherto unheard of in the long and august tradition of tequila distillery. The Mexican tequila producers were not prepared to take this assault on their reputation lying down. After a few years, Grassl was forced to give up his enterprise.

Guadalajara – mariachis, horsemen and tequila

Getting there and when to travel
Air: from Mexico City to Guadalajara.
Bus, car and train: from Guadalajara on the highway to Tepic until the exit for Tequila. The famous tequila-express leaves from Guadalajara and takes about 1.5 hours to reach the little town of Amititán, where the Hacienda San José del Regufio produces the world-famous Teqila Herradura.
Best travel time: all year.

Where to stay
****Villa Ganz. Villa built in colonial style with ten generous rooms furnished with antiques. Cozy lobby with open fireplace, beautiful garden. López Cotilla 1739. Toll-free tel: 01-800/5 08 79, e-mail: villaganz@mexicoboutiquehotels.com, www.mexicoboutiquehotels.com/villaganz

*****Hotel Camino Real Guadalajara. Big luxury hotel in the picturesque suburb of Zapopan. Modern architecture, contemporary art. Av. Vallarta No. 5505. Tel: 33/31 34 24 24, fax: 31 34 24 04, toll-free domestic number: 01/800/901 23 00, e-mail: Guadalajara@caminoreal.com.mx, www.caminoreal.com/guadalajara

Must see
International Mariachi and Charro Festivals, both in fall.
Horse-drawn coach rides through historic Guadalajara.
Procession of Our Virgin of Zapopan on October 12.
The procession is the highlight of the miracle-working saint's "journey" that begins on June 13 and "visits" the churches in Guadalajara on its route.

Local attractions
Zapopan: important pilgrimage site, about 7 km (4 miles) northwest of the center. Founded in 1542 by Franciscan friars. The former monastery, the baroque basilica, and the museum featuring Huichol folk art are worth visiting.
Tlaquepaque: picturesque little town to the southeast of Guadalajara. Center for local arts and crafts (ceramics, glass, paper maché figures). Very attractive zócalo, where mariachis and tequila combine to create a great atmosphere.
The Museo Regional de la Cerámica in a former 19th-century manor is worth a visit.

Information
Secretaria de Turismo des Estado de Jaliscso (Setujal), Morelos No. 102. Tel: 33/36 68 18 00.

Hot on the Heels of the Wild West's Heroes
Durango – the Treasure of the Sierra Madre

The past comes alive in Durango. The state in the north of Mexico is rich in natural resources and blessed with a varied landscape that has served as a backdrop for countless Hollywood films.

It is a quiet morning. A deep blue sky stretches over our heads. The wind whistles through deserted streets and blows sand into our eyes. A wooden door creaks and the gallows wait quietly for their victim. There is nobody far or wide. Only bare mountains on the horizon. No voices, no music in the saloon. Any second now, a shot is sure to fall and a horde of bandits will appear from their ambush to rob us of our earthly goods.

We are in the village of Chupaderos, taking in the same air that Raoul Walsh, John Wayne, and Charles Bronson breathed before us. We left nearby Durango early – so that we could get a real taste of the atmosphere here. The village, with its small churches and stables, has served as location for many films: revolution and the Mexican-American War have played out in this town. Pancho Villa, hero of the revolution, came back to life here. Another film town is situated not far away: Cañón de los Delgado, especially constructed in 1997 for the film One Man's Hero, takes us back to 1860. Film fever has us in its thrall now as we travel on to the Ranch La Joya where Bandidos, with Salma Hayek and Penelope Cruz, was made. In that film, the splendid Ricardo Castro theater in Durango served as the bank that was robbed by the beautiful Mexican actress, whilst the Zambrano Palace was the background for her spectacular escape. The Museo Temático de Cine in Durango has exhibits from over 50 years of film history in Durango: cameras and furniture, costumes, film posters, backdrops, even whole sets and outfits worn by the stars can be admired here.

The hero of the revolution, Pancho Villa, came from Durango. He committed his first murder at the tender age of 16, when he killed the son of a wealthy landowner to avenge the sullied honor of his sister. He fled to Chihuahua and changed his name to Francisco

1 Walking paradise, Sierra de los Organos National Park near Durango.
2 Wild West à la Mexicana.
3 Bandit, revolutionary, and national hero from Durango: statue of Pancho Villa in Parral.
4 On the trail of John Wayne: Hollywood backdrop for a western town in Durango.

1 Not play-acting but real life: cowboy in the Sierra de los Organos in Durango.
2 Lava and basalt rocks form a natural backdrop for countless westerns.
3 The past comes alive: daily western show in Villa del Oeste near Durango.
4 Charles Bronson was an early fan: can-can dancers in the Villa del Oeste.
5 Almost as it was during the gold rush: the Hostal de la Mina in Somberete.

"Pancho" Villa. He was a real outlaw, glorified as a freedom fighter in many films: Mexico's Robin Hood. The capital city, officially named Durango de Victoria, is situated in the fertile Guadiana valley. Father Diego de la Cadena founded a settlement here in 1556. The town was given its name in 1563 but was known late into the 18th century only as Villa de Guadiana. The Spanish conquistadors met with bitter resistance on the part of the pre-Spanish population, the half nomadic tribes of Tepehuano and Acaxe, whose descendaents still live in remote villages in the Sierra Madre. Fighting between the two parties continued for a long time. Peace in the region, which, together with Chihuahua, comprised the province of Nueva Vizcaya was not established until the 18th century. Durango became a bishopric and was finally declared regional capital in 1823 when the Durango region separated from Chihuahua and become a separate state. Economic prosperity did not come until the 20th century.

The film business brought many fans here, above all from the United States, but tourism continued to play a relatively minor role and the town kept its provincial atmosphere. When evening falls, the town puts on a different face and turns into a splendid sight. The warm light that falls from the old street lanterns emphasizes the majestic beauty of the baroque and neoclassical buildings from

the colonial era. The best time to take the "Tranvía Turístico" for a trip through the historic center is the afternoon (Wednesdays through Sundays from 17-21). The bars and restaurants in the old walls begin to fill up – especially around the Plaza Santa Ana. In the Mi Viejo Barrio bar, young people meet up before heading off into the evening. The Méson de Santa Ana restaurant is an ideal place to nourish body and soul and soak up some Mexican atmosphere. The cuisine in the Fonda Tía and La Casa de Teja (Hotel Casablanca) restaurants is legendary.

Durango is Mexico's third-largest state. The mountains are home to huge reserves of gold, silver, copper, iron, tin, lead, sulphur, and antimony. In the fertile areas around Gómez Palacio, cotton, tobacco, wheat, corn, sugarcane and, lately, also wine are cultivated. The cotton harvest and late summer vintage are the occasion for numerous local festivals. Mapimí National Park is situated in the north, named for the eponymous mining town.

Nature lovers, mountaineers, and mountain bikers (still) find it worth their while to make their way to Sierra de los Organos, south of Durango on the way to Somberete. Huge rocks and chasms made of lava and basalt coupled with a unique vegetation promise exceptional experiences. There are no huts here, no snack kiosks on parking lots to disturb the magnificent scenery. The sun's journey across the sky provides a fantastic spectacle of light and shade – no wonder that Hollywood found an ideal backdrop here for the resurrection of the Wild, Wild West.

Durango – on the heels of the Wild West's heroes

Getting there and when to travel
Air: from Mexico City.
Bus and car: from the north via Monterrey, Saltillo, and Toréon (toll highway), from Zacatecas to the south via the highway until just after Fresnillo: from there, turn off onto route Mex 45. There is a stunningly beautiful but very curvy road that goes from Mazatlán on the Pacific coast through the Sierra Madre to Durango.
Best travel time: all year. The region is particularly beautiful in the spring, when the fruit trees (peaches) are in flower and in late summer.

Where to stay
****Hotel Posada San Jorge*, Constitución 102 Sur, center. Tel: 618/813 32 57, fax: 811 60 40, e-mail: informacion@hotelposadasanjorge.com.mx, www.hotelposadosanjorge.com.mx
****Hotel Gobernador*, Av. 20 de Noviembre 257 Ote., center. Tel: 618/813 19 19, e-mail: hgreservaciones@infosel.net.mx
****Hotel de la Monja*, Constitución 214, center. Tel: 618/837 17 19, fax: 837 17 24
***Hostal de la Mina in Somberete*. Simple hotel on the outskirts of the town. Ideal for overnight stays on the way to Zacatecas. Somberete is a very pretty mining town. Tel: 433/935 03 44

Must see
Vineyard mass in Gómez Palacio (end of August, beginning of September) and vintages in the surrounding villages.

Local attractions
Cerro del Mercado in the northwest of the capital, site of one of the most important hematite mines in Mexico.
Guadalupe town with the house of Mexico's first President, General "Gaudillo" Guadalupe Victoria (1786–1843), on the River Tamazula.
Villa del Oeste, former western village, now a theme park with western shows, 12 km (7 miles) in the direction of Parral, open Tuesday through Sunday, 12–15.
La Ferreria: archeological site 7 km (4 miles) south of Durango in the direction of Lerdo de Tejeda. Worth seeing: hunting scenes engraved in stone, several buildings, the (hardly recognizable) ballcourt and the main pyramid.

Information
Información Turística, on the corner of Florida and Av. 20 de Noviembre. Tel: 618/714 15 56, www.durango.gob.mx

Mexico's Colonial Past
Zacatecas – Lagos de Moreno – Guanajuato

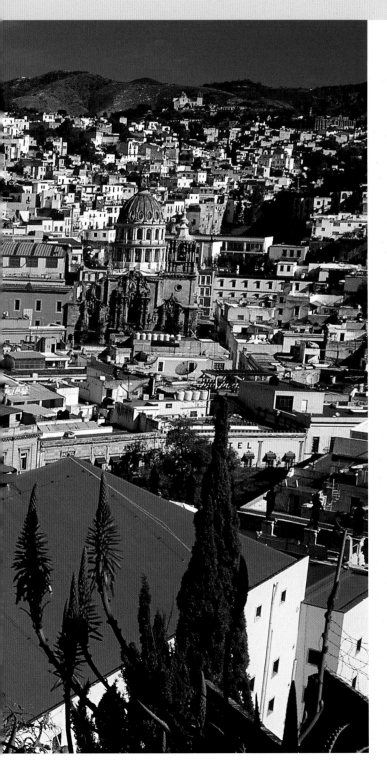

They testify to the immense wealth of the colonial masters from Spain: the cities of Zacatecas, Guanajuato, and Lagos de Moreno in the central highlands of Mexico. The ups and downs of Mexico's history are still in evidence here.

Like many of its colonial sisters, the city of Zacatecas, capital of the eponymous state, is a UNESCO World Heritage Site. But of all those cities in Latin America, Zacatecas is considered the best preserved. Its name in Náhuatl is derived from "zacate" and means "place of abundant zacates" – a plant that is cultivated for cattle fodder and is also used to make brooms and brushes. Visitors to Zacatecas will immediately notice its two hills: La Bufa, with the huge monument for the revolutionary hero Pancho Villa on its summit, and El Grillo. They are connected by cable car. La Bufa is the city symbol and forms part of the region's coat of arms. The cobbled streets are peaceful. No glaring advertising hoardings despoil the majestic architecture. Delicate, wrought-iron balconies lend the town a cheerful demeanor.

Zacatecas was founded in 1546, after Spaniards had discovered huge silver reserves nearby. They built magnificent palaces and wide-stepped alleys, shady arcades and splendid churches. The cathedral is a masterwork of baroque church architecture. Its main façade is covered with a patchwork of delicate motifs.

Opposite the cathedral, little Venya alley takes us to Santo Domingo Church and to the Museum Rafael Coronel, a former Franciscan monastery from the 18th century. The artist bequeated his collection of about 10,000 Mexican masks to the city of his birth. In addition to his own paintings, his private collection of Mexican arts and crafts is also on show alongside sketches by the great fresco painter Diego Rivera and pre-Hispanic objects. The town has Rafael's brother Pedro to thank for one of the best museums of modern art in Mexico. The Pedro Coronel Museum

1 Charro riders in the traditional hacienda Sepúlveda in Lagos de Moreno.
2 Silver from the hills of Zacatecas.
3 Sweet and juicy: the fruit of the Nopal cactus, locally known as "tunas".
4 The most beautiful view over Guanajuato belongs to the national hero "El Pipila" and his monument.
The miner was one of the leaders in the first battle for Mexican independence in Guanajuato, 1810.

has work by Pablo Picasso, George Braque, Salvador Dalí, Marc Chagall, and Basarelli. The library, with about 20,000 volumes from the 16th to the 19th century, is amazing.

Another internationally renowned artist from Zacateca is Manual Felguérez. The museum of the same name that he bequeathed to the city is housed in a 19th-century building and has a comprehensive collection of abstract art from the last 50 years. Another of the city's famous sons, the artist Francisco Goitía, also has a museum that bears his name. It is located in a French-style villa that served as the Governor's Mansion until 1962. In addition to work by Goitía himself, it shows work by other Zacatecan artists such as Felguérez, the Coronel brothers, Julio Ruelas, and José Kuri. The Huichol Indians have maintained their cultural independence for centuries. The area in which they settled includes Nayarit, parts of Jalisco and Zacatecas, Durango, and San Luis Potosí, where their holy mountain Wirikuta is situated not far from the legendary mining city, Real de Catorce. They are famous for their colorful beaded embroidery. A particularly magnificent example is on show in the Zacatecas Museum: it was commissioned by a Belgian doctor called Mertens, who specified payment in kind but not with the usual chickens and donkeys. Instead, he bought the Indians four different colored threads and asked them to embroider their own religious symbols. The result outshone all his expectations and formed the ground stone of a unique collection that he later gave to the town. It is worth visiting the city just to see it.

In fact, you need more than one day to see all the sights in Zacatecas. After we had visited the majestic Teatro Calderón, built between 1891 and 1897, and seen the aqueduct that dates from the end of the 18th century, as well as some of the churches and palaces along the way, it seems a good time to go back to our delightful Hotel Mesón de Jobito, by Juárez Park.

The hotel was built in the mid-19th century as a hostel for travelers and later served as "vecindad" for many families. During the day, the women would meet here to gossip; in the evenings and on

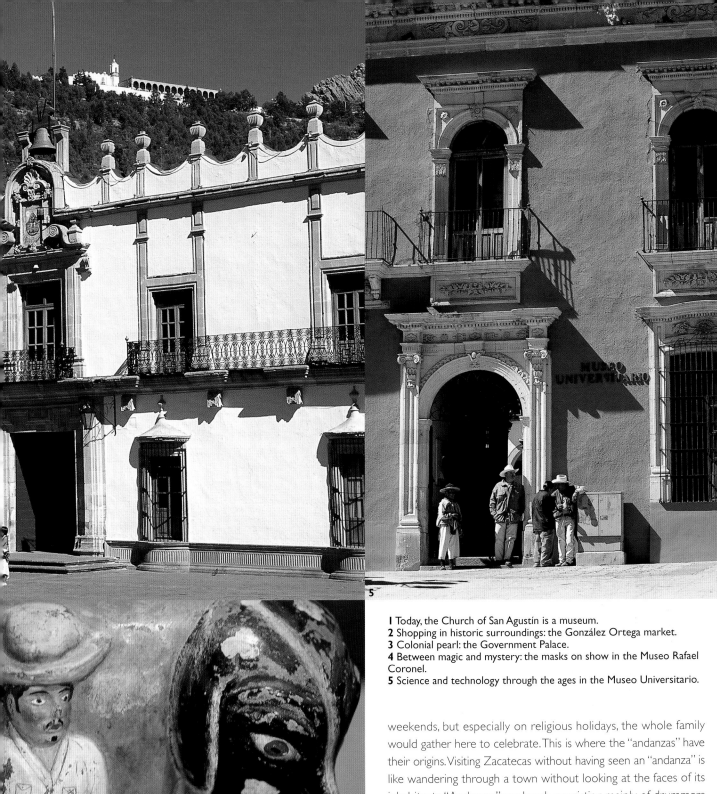

1 Today, the Church of San Agustín is a museum.
2 Shopping in historic surroundings: the González Ortega market.
3 Colonial pearl: the Government Palace.
4 Between magic and mystery: the masks on show in the Museo Rafael Coronel.
5 Science and technology through the ages in the Museo Universitario.

weekends, but especially on religious holidays, the whole family would gather here to celebrate. This is where the "andanzas" have their origins. Visiting Zacatecas without having seen an "andanza" is like wandering through a town without looking at the faces of its inhabitants. "Andanzas" are bands consisting mainly of drummers who wind their way through the old town of an evening to the sound of loud drum rolls (called "tamborazos," which comes from "tambor," the word for drum).

"El Tamborazo" is a tradition started by miners in the early 17th century. Acoustically, it imitates the sound of hammers on stone. Other instruments, such as trumpets, were added later. Young men

1 Whets the appetite: the Mercado Hidalgo in Guanajuato.
2 Flower sellers on the Plaza del Daratillo in Guanajuato.
3 From a Spanish colony to independence: the fresco of José Chávez Morado in the Museum of Alhóndiga de Granaditos.

used to meet in the "vecindad" on Saturday afternoons to ring in the weekend. They would go from one family to the next, collect their tips (raya) and play. More and more people would join in as the evening progressed until a large group had come together, moving through the streets, making music, and celebrating. Even today, the first tune is the "Zacatecas March." Before the procession starts, the musicians hand out little clay jugs attached to ribbons to the onlookers, who hang them around their necks. One of the musicians leads a donkey and cart with jugs full of Mezcal, a liqueur made from agaves. No wonder that the atmosphere improves from one street corner to the next.

A trip in the cable car is an absolute must for visitors to Zacatecas. The starting point is either El Grillo or La Bufa. The best time for such an outing is late afternoon, when the setting sun picks out the fading contours so clearly that everything appears sharply focused,

close enough to touch. At La Bufa there is also an entrance to the underground mine of El Edén. A small railway takes visitors deep inside the mountain. At the end of the line a reward awaits the young and the young at heart: the disco El Malacate.

The captivating little town of Lagos de Moreno lies on the road from Zacatecas via Aguascalientes to Guanajuato on the Río San Juan. Its beauty is the result of wealth accumulated by the Spanish cattle barons, horse breeders, and arable farmers. The area is very fertile. Both cereals and wine are grown here. Splendid haciendas still bear witness to the prosperity of these property owners. For a long time, this region lay far off the tourist track. These days the thermal springs, the reservoir lakes at El Cuarenta and La Sauceda, the Sierra de Comanja, and the Mesa Redonda are especially popular with visitors from near and far.

The city, founded in 1563 as "La Villa de Santa María de los Lagos" on the historic silver barons' "King's Highway" from Zacatecas to Guanajuato and Mexico City, was once the site of bloody battles between Spaniards and the indigenous population – a tribe called the Guachichiles known for its bellicosity – who vehemently opposed the Spanish invaders for a long time. But even after the Spanish conquest, Lagos de Moreno retained a key position as a result of its strategic location. No less than 17 uprisings were registered in Jalisco between 1855 and 1864. Lagos de Moreno enjoyed temporary status as capital city of the state in the period between 1829 and 1916. The town's name derives from its hero: Pedro Romero (1775–1817), leader of a successful uprising.

Lagos de Moreno earned its reputation as the "Athens of Bajío" (the region is sometimes also called Bajío) during the reign of the dictator Porfirio Díaz, who ruled over the country from 1876 until the outbreak of the revolution in 1910. During the Porfiriat, the colonial towns were enriched with many splendid buildings in the French style. The architecture, the fashion, and the lifestyle were all strongly influenced by Paris – in Lagos de Moreno as elsewhere. A good example is the José Rosas Moreno theater.

Another impressive example of colonial architecture is the cathedral with its two slim spires whose late baroque ornamentation verges on the excessive. The façade is a particularly good example of the Churrigueresque style: the mixture of Indian and the

1 The "Athens of Bajío," Lagos de Moreno.
2 Ornamentation hewn from pink marble: the late baroque façade of the Cathedral of Lagos de Moreno.
3 Courtyard of the former monastery and sometime residence of the independence hero Father Miguel Hidalgo.
4 The dome of the Cathedral Nuestra Señora de Asunción.

European art of decoration. Lagos de Moreno has many churches and former monasteries, some of which have splendid courtyards and gardens. One of these is the historic Rinconada de la Merced, where Mexico's hero of independence, the priest Miguel Hidalgo, stayed during his sojourns in the city.

Porfirio Diáz brought industrial progress to the country – but it was achieved on the backs of the innumerable and impoverished peasants and workers. The great haciendas reached the zenith of their magnificence during this era. Two examples are the San Rafael and the Sepúlveda haciendas. The former dates to the 19th century and is a rustic-style hotel today. A visit here takes you back to

the heyday of hacienda life: most of the rooms still have their original furnishings.

The Sepúlveda hacienda is even older: Spaniard Don Juan de Sepúlveda began tilling the soil here more than 360 years ago. Today, the hacienda is a premium-class luxury hotel complete with its own lake, 11 suites and a small wellness center. Juan Alonso Serrano, the hotel director, invested ten years and a lot of money in a painstaking restoration that has turned the building into a real jewel. The romantic restaurant serves an exquisite regional cuisine prepared by Mariquita, who has been cooking for the family for over 30 years. The hotel has its own horses and offers horseback excursions into the beautiful surroundings.

"Ay Guanajuato de mis amores" (Ah, Guanajuato, most beloved of my loves) is the title of a local song, and once you've been to the town, you'll know what it refers to: the capital city of the state that bears the same name is a jewel of colonial architecture. Guanajuato, the city that hosts the International Cervantes Festival,

was declared a UNESCO World Heritage Site in 1988. Since May 2005, Guanajuato also bears the title "Cervantes Capital of the American Continent," awarded by the UNESCO center in Castilla-La Mancha in Spain.

Guanajuato is the only city in the world that honors the Spanish writer Miguel del Cervantes y Saavedra with his own festival as well as dedicating an entire museum to his tragic hero, Don Quixote. What began 50 years ago as "Entremeses Cervantinos" has now grown into one of the world's most important festivals of theater, literature, and music. Famous stage ensembles, authors, and orchestras come here every year in October and transform the picturesque squares and courtyards in the colonial buildings into a huge open-air theater.

Situated on the slopes of Mount Cubilete, the town owes its beauty to a rich vein of gold and silver that the Spaniards discovered here in the 16th century. The "La Valenciana" mine is no longer in production today, but can still be visited. The impressive

1 350 years of history: the Hacienda Sepúlveda near Lagos de Moreno is one of the oldest and most beautiful haciendas in Mexico.
2 Once a "vecindad" for the poor, the Méson de Jobita in Zacatecas now houses a luxury hotel with suites for affluent tourists.
3 Cozy and romantic: the Hacienda San Rafael near Lagos de Moreno.
4 and 5 Ideal for some privacy: patio and pool of the Hacienda Sepúlveda.

church on the hillside above the city was named San Cayetano but is only ever called "La Valenciana." Its blue dome rises majestically into the sky. The view from here onto the city is especially beautiful in the late afternoon and particularly so in January and February when the huge jacaranda trees shroud Valenciana in a pale lilac veil of blossom.

Guanajuato is also a synonym for romance. Narrow alleys wind their way past houses painted in delicate shades of pastel colors with intricately wrought balconies. There are flowerpots and window boxes everywhere, often filled with magnificent specimens of bougainvillea. Every couple wants to seal their love with a kiss in the "Callejón del Beso" (Alley of Kisses), on the exact spot where an unhappy couple à la Romeo and Juliet once met for a clandestine kiss. The alley is so narrow that lovers can almost reach out and touch each other from balcony to balcony. And whilst

Zacatecas is famous for its andanzas, Guanajuato has its "estudiantinas," groups of students dressed in local costumes that roam through the city streets and cafés, singing, making music, and spreading good cheer. As was the case with Zacatecas, Lagos de Moreno, and Dolores Hidalgo, the city played a major role in

Mexico's long road to independence. The first great battle in the War of Independence was fought on the Alhóndiga de Granaditas. Today it is the site of the regional history museum. The Plaza de la Paz and the Jardín de la Unión belong to the most beautiful spots in the city. There is no better place to indulge in some people-watching.

A second testament to the immense wealth of the silver barons is situated outside the city walls: the hacienda San Gabriel de Barrera. It is also worth visiting the house that Mexico's most famous fresco painter, Diego Rivera, lived and worked in. The birthplace of the well-known singer Jorge Negrete is not far away. He remains an idol for all Mexicans, young and old, decades after his death.

There is slightly less romance in the air of the Museum of Mummies: getting there on foot is difficult – a steep upward walk through narrow alleys. Once you have arrived, you'll need to be patient before you are allowed to see the bodies, well preserved in clay earth, that were taken from a former graveyard. The queue of expectant visitors is long, whatever time of day you come. It's best to bring along something to drink, as well as sun protection, if you don't want to suffer from exposure to heat and sun.

Zacatecas – Mexico's colonial past

Getting there and when to travel
Air: direct from Mexico City to Zacatecas and Guanajuato. The airport closest to Lagos de Moreno is Léon.
Bus and car: Mex 57 Highway from Mexico City to Quéretaro, via Mex 45 to Lagos de Moreno and on to Zacatecas. After Irapuato, turn off for Guanajuato. Alternatively, take the Mex 57 from Quéretaro, San Miguel de Allende, and Dolores Hidalgo. Regular bus service throughout the day from all major cities.
Best travel time: November to June.

Where to stay
*****Méson de Jobito*, delightful hotel in the historic center. Jardín Juárez no 143, 98000 Zacatecas. Tel: 924/35 00, e-mail: ventas@mesondejobito.com, www.mesondejobito.com
*****Hacienda Sepúlveda*, luxury hotel in historic walls, Carretera Lagos-El Puesto km 6 (4 miles), 47400 Lagos de Moreno. Tel: 01-800/508 79 23, e-mail: Sepulveda@mexicoboutiquehotels.com, www.mexicoboutiquehotels,com/sepulveda

***Quinta Las Acacias*, Boutique hotel in a former town palace not far from the city center. Paseo de la Presa 163, 36000 Guanajuato. Tel: 731/15 17, fax 731/18 62, e-mail: quintalasacacias@prodigy.net.mx, www.quintalasacacias.com
****Real de Minas*. Hotel outside the historic center of Guanajuato with beautiful gardens, Nejayote No. 17. Tel: 732/14 60, 732/18 36, e-mail: realminas@guanajuato-touristico.com

Must see
Día de la Morismo, August 27, Zacatecas, when the battle between Spaniards and Moors is reenacted.
Fiesta Nuestra Señora del Patrocino, September 14, Zacatecas. Processions and sacrificial gifts.
Independence celebrations, September 15, in Zacatecas.
Festival Cervantino in Guanajuato, October. Early hotel reservations advisable.

Information
Oficina de Turismo, Av. Hidalgo No. 401, 98999 Zacatecas. Tel: 925/12 77
Lagos de Moreno: www.lagosdemoreno.gob.mx
Secretaría de Turismo de Guanajuato, Plaza de la Paz No. 14, 36000 Guanajuato. Tel: 732/15 74, 732/76 87, e-mail: turismo@guanajuatacapital.com, www.guanajuato.gob.mx

The North Beach of the Isla Mujeres.

The South of Mexico

Pictures from the Paris of Mexico
The Luxury of Mérida, a Trip to Uxmal

"The White City": with its colonial splendor and its magnificent palaces built by the sisal barons, Mérida is regarded as the queen of the cities on the Yucatán peninsula. It is characterized by Caribbean flair, joie de vivre, and the cheerful temperament of its inhabitants.

The land is flat, the soil is dry and full of lime, the sun beats down mercilessly, and the wind whistles. Not what one normally calls idyllic. But there were times when valuable goods sailed into the port of Sisal that serves this inhospitable region: marble, porcelain, silk and brocade, gold-framed mirror – all from Europe and all for Mexico.

These luxurious goods traveled over land into the heart of the state of Yucatán. In the course of the 19th century, its beautiful capital city of Mérida gradually gained a reputation as the Paris of Mexico. The luxury was acquired with the help of a natural product manufactured in the coastal region of Yucatán: the henequen fiber that turned into Mexico's No. 1 export hit. The henequen agaves delivered the best natural material for ropes and rigging, for which there was great demand in the war-torn Europe of the early 20th century. Since the European and North American buyers had great difficulty in pronouncing the word henequen, the plant was simply called by the name of the harbor from which it was exported – sisal – and became world-famous under the nickname of "green gold."

In those days, there were haciendas all over the country, yet they were regarded not so much as representative residential abodes but as places dominated by the laws of hard work and profit. Festivities took place elsewhere: in Mérida, the newly-enriched plantation owners created a forum to display their wealth – with villas, theaters, and broad boulevards.

Mérida may be beautiful but with over one million inhabitants it is also fairly big. We prefer the peace and quiet of the Hacienda Xcanatun. Built in the 18th century, it served as home to a family of cattle ranchers, corn barons, and sisal plantation owners. In 1984, the hacienda was sold to the Ruz-Baker family who reopened it as a hotel with 18 spacious suites in ample and quietly idyllic garden surroundings. The old water tank was turned into a

1 A relaxing massage in a tropical setting on the Hacienda Xcanatun.
2 The classic Mexican cocktail: a margarita.
3 A tower crowns the façade of the Palacio Municipal in Mérida.
4 The Spanish named this building in Uxmal the "Nuns' House.

pool whilst the restaurant Casa la Piedra was installed in the machine room, where the cook concocts regional delicacies such as lime soup or "Puc Chuc," the traditional piglet with Seville oranges (an Indian combination), which has become famous throughout the region and beyond. The healing powers of Mayan medicine can be tested in the hotel's private wellness area, from aloe vera masks to honey blossom massages. A further advantage: trips to the sights of north Yucatán can be easily arranged from this starting point.

Whilst the city expanded outwards, the center of Mérida kept its colonial character with a symmetrical chess board arrangement of numbered streets. The main square – not referred to here as zócalo but as the Plaza Mayor – is fronted by the cathedral and an eggshell-colored town hall whose façade is decorated with double rows of arcades and a three-tiered tower. It dates back to the 18th century. The frescoes in the Government Palace (Palacio del Gobierno) to the north of the Plaza are painted morality tales on the evils of the unbridled prosperity enjoyed by the henequen dealers: the artist, José Castro Pacheco, depicted the forced labor to which the Mayas were subjected in the fields. The oldest house in Yucatán, the Casa de Montejo, is situated on the southern edge

1 The Kukulcan pyramid in Chichén Itzá: its nine terraces represent nine heavens and have four sets of stairs facing nouth, south, east, and west, each with 91 steps totaling 365 days if the platform is included. The head of a serpent reposes at the foot of each flight of stairs. Every year, on September 21, the natural play of light and shade forms a serpent that winds its way down from top to toe.
2 The Gubernatorial Palace in Uxmal.
3 – 4 The Mayan sites of Sayil and Dzibilchatún.
5 The former Franciscan monastery in Izamal is the biggest in Latin America.

fantastic palaces and temples. Findings from the cenote (known as "d'zenots" in the Mayan language to refer to natural sinkholes that have opened up in the limestone high above the sea) in Chichén Itzá are on view alongside Mayan codices copied out by Spanish monks.

Mayan hieroglyphics comprise 800 signs, one half of which took the form of syllables; the remainder consisted of whole words. About 85 percent of these have been deciphered and are legible. The texts tell us that the use of written language was a privilege reserved for the ruling classes. They dealt with religious rituals and customs as well as historic events. Stele and statues are adorned with written explanations; writing materials consisted of the bark of trees soaked in calf's milk, as well as ceramics and wood. Much has been destroyed: the Spanish conquistadors thought it expedient to burn such vehicles of heathen belief.

If you are looking for a folksy contrast to the historic Mérida there is no better place to go to than the market which spreads itself over several streets in the area between Calles 54–58 and 65–69. There is no shortage of beautiful arts and crafts products. The exquisitely coiffed and bejeweled Mayan women with their colorfully embroidered white tunics have an additional attraction on offer: the handwoven hammocks in all the colors of the rainbow. They are considered the best that money can buy – and not only in Mexico itself.

Those unwilling to try out the regional cuisine on the market will be well taken care of in the Belle Epoque restaurant on the Plaza Mayor, especially if they take a table on the first-floor balconies. For a long time, Mérida was merely a rural town surrounded only by haciendas. Its development on the periphery, independent of Mexico City, resulted in a typically regional cuisine such as the "cochinito pibil," or roast piglet with grilled leeks. But eating a local specialty is really only the beginning of an evening's entertainment à la meridéña. The town is proud of its artistic reputation: hardly an evening passes without a folkloristic ballet performed in the Parque Santa Lucía or concerts given at local venues.

It is tempting to stay in the hacienda idyll Xcanatun and just relax

of the Plaza. It was home to the conqueror of the Maya, Francisco Montejo, who had his bloodthirsty deeds immortalized in stone engravings: Spaniards trampling on Indians can be seen over the entrance.

The Museo de Antropología e Historia on Paseo Montejo is a welcome source of information on the magical world of Mayan civilization that will come in useful for our later visits to their

1 Impressive country estate in tranquil surroundings: the Hacienda Xcanatun.
2 A view inside: more understated luxury.
3 A hacienda terrace.
4 Luxurious bath in one of the master suites in Xcanatun.
5 A painting from colonial times decorates one of the rooms in the Hacienda Temozón.

but a visit to magnificent Uxmal is definitely worthwhile. A sea of softly undulating hills ("puuc" in Mayan) stretches away to the south of Mérida, overgrown with dense bushes. After about 80 kilometers (50 miles), Uxmal appears on the horizon. It was built in the 7th century by emigrants from Petén (in what is Guatemala today). From the 9th century onwards, the Maya tribe of Xiú lived there until they moved on six centuries later. They built most of the palaces and buildings that still exist today. So Uxmal remains the home of the most beautiful testaments to the Puuc style: geometric stone mosaics that spread over façades in patterns comprising hundreds of triangles, meanders, circles, and squares. And because there is such an abundance of ornamentation, the style is called Mayan Baroque, even if this symphony of straight lines is not a feature normally associated with European Baroque. The symbol that occurs most frequently in Uxmal is Chaac, the god of rain, recognizable by his trunk nose. A quick look around at

the uneven and prickly green of the surrounding bushes from which the temple platforms arise makes it clear that this is a region in need of rain – and one in which a rain god would have dominated the strictly ordered pantheon of Mayan gods.

The Pirámide del Adivino, or Fortune-teller's Pyramid, is particularly rich in Chaac masks. Narrow stairs lead up from an oval foundation to a vertiginous height of 38 meters (125 feet); five temples are situated in the temple's interior.

In the "Nuns' House" opposite the Fortune-teller's Pyramid, four wings from different building epochs frame a central courtyard, achieving an unexpectedly harmonious effect. Of course, the building has nothing to do with nuns; it was probably just the many doors in the building's façade that reminded the Spaniards of convent architecture. The walls are smooth but richly decorated above the portals with stone masks, Mayan huts, Chaac symbols, monkeys, and birds. After crossing a paved ball court, visitors will reach the House of Turtles, on whose cornices beautiful stone turtles are positioned. The house is also dedicated to the rain god Chaac. The impressive Gubernatorial Palace is located nearby with its numerous entrances and a 100-meter-long (330 feet) façade covered with ornamental friezes. The architect Frank Lloyd Wright once described it as America's most perfect building.

Mérida and Uxmal – the Paris of Mexico

Getting there and when to travel
Air: various Mexican airlines connect Mérida with Mexico City, Acapulco, Oaxaca and Cancún.
Bus: first-class terminal in Calle 70/69 and 71. Second-class terminal Calle 68/69 and 70. Connections to Mexico City, Chetumal, Campeche, Palenque, Veracruz, and Villahermosa, including Cancún, Chichén Iztá, Uxmal, and Valladolid.
Best travel time: all year around. It is always warm. Rainy season from August to October.

Where to stay
*****Hacienda Xcanatun*. Tel: 999/941 02 13, www.xcanatun.com, stylishly restored former sisal hacienda set in magnificent surroundings. Good location for all

excursions to local attractions in the region. The Casa La Piedra Restaurant has a very good reputation.
*****La Casa del Balam*, Calle 60/57. Tel: 999/924 21 50, fax: 924 50 11, elegant colonial-style hotel in the town center, 60 generously designed rooms and suites, garden.
*** Posada Toledo, Calle 58, No. 487. Tel: 999/923 16 90, fax: 923 22 56, an airy colonial house built around a courtyard, redesigned as inexpensive lodgings in the city center. Beautiful restaurant.

Must see
Museo Regional de Antropología e Historia, Palacio Cantón, Paseo de Montejo. Other museums of note: Museo de Arte Contemporáneo on the Plaza, Museo de Arte Popular, Calle 59/60, Parque Mejorada, Museo de la Canción Yucateca, Calle 63/66, Museo de la Ciudad, small local history museum Calle 61/58.
Numerous open-air folklore concerts and ballet performances in parks and in the Teatro Peón Contreras.

Local Attractions
Uxmal: Immerse yourself in the world of the Maya. To the south of Uxmal: Kabah, Sayil, Xlapak, and Labná with important palaces and buildings that exemplify the *Puuc style*.
Halfway between Mérida and Cancún: Ek Balam, with its huge palace and almost perfectly preserved stucco decorations that were long hidden under a hill.

Information
Teatro Peón Contreras, Calle 60/57 for tourist information. www.yucatan.gob.mx

The Island of Women
Languorous Days on the Isla Mujeres

The beaches are straight from paradise – gleaming, fine, white sand and a sea of azure blue that could not be more beautiful: Isla Mujeres. The small "Island of Women," just off Cancún's coast, not only promises a picture postcard idyll. It also delivers one.

As flat as a fish and generously covered with macchia bushes, eight kilometers (5 miles) long and not more than 500 meters (1,650 feet) wide – such is the Isla Mujeres. Salt flats and a lagoon run through the island and with the rough winds that batter its northern, sea-facing coastline, it does not conform to average tourist expectations. But perhaps it is precisely this rough and ready charm that makes it so attractive.

On Avenida Hidalgo, we rent a small moped – only two wheels are allowed here so it is this or a bicycle to explore the island. The Avenida is the pedestrian zone and this is where most of the tourist industry is based – in the many bars and restaurants. The Isla Mujeres – Island of Women – gets its name from Francisco Hernández de Córdoba, who came here in 1517 with an expedition and found numerous female clay images among the Mayan ruins. Most of the temples were probably dedicated to the goddess Ix Chel. One of them still stands on the island's southernmost point today. It is a 15-minute trip by moped. In former times, the Indians came here on pilgrimages to worship the goddess of fertility and the moon. The temple dates back to the 10th century.

Although you should not come to the Isla Mujeres looking for heavenly calm, there is far less commotion and party life here than in Cancún. The beaches are flat, the water clear. On our way to the southernmost tip, we stop for a look at the legendary Hacienda Mundaca. The infamous slave trader and pirate Fermín Mundaca built it in 1860. He forced rebellious Mayas to destroy their own temples and build this hacienda with the selfsame stones.

As an older man, Mundaca fell in love with a young girl. However, she failed to return his feelings. He called her La Trigüena and had the words "Paso de la Trigüena" engraved over the entrance to the

1 You will feel at home with Lisa and César at Elements of the Island, Isla Mujeres.
2 Still life with hammocks, Isla Mujeres.
3 On the outskirts of Isla Mujeres.
4 So far and yet so near: Cancún seen from the Casa de los Sueños.

...nda. The old man seems to have lost his mind over this ...requited love. It is said that he died lonely and confused in Mérida. The Hacienda Mundaca with its exotic gardens and nesting places for birds has been restored and expanded to include a small zoo. Hacienda and zoo are open to the public. Going southwards, they can be found about 3.5 kilometers (2 miles) to the north of Playa Lancheros and Playa Paraíso.

The Ecopark Garrafón nature reserve in the southwestern corner of the island includes a coral reef (albeit extinct) and offers many attractive snorkeling opportunities. Day-trippers often come over from Cancún for a change of scenery. All the hubbub does not seem to bother the wide variety of fishes. Barracudas, parrot fishes, small sharks, and perch have been sighted here. Those who prefer their dusky perch or horse mackerel served up grilled on a plate are entitled to hope for a selection of the freshest fish available in the local restaurants. A good example is the Garrafón de Castilla, the restaurant in the park's service center that also features a snack bar, showers, and sun-beds – everything you might need to

spend a pleasant day relaxing. For those who want to spend more time in natural surroundings, an enclosure has been established in Sac Bajo to provide a safe haven for sea turtles. Since 1990, it has been forbidden to hunt turtles for meat or for their shells. Now, they can lay their eggs in the warm sand of Isla Mujeres, watched over by trained staff, who place the eggs in hatching pans. The baby turtles live in a special enclosure until they are old enough to be liberated by local children, whose privilege it is to watch them crawl slowly to freedom.

It is not clear whether the fertility goddess Ix Chel or the unhappy passion of Señor Mundaca inspired the Isla Mujeres to advertise itself as a destination for honeymooners. Some accommodations, such as the large, modern Avalón Hotel, provide special services for the newly-married. The Casa de los Sueños, situated on the beach at the northern tip of the island, provides a more individual getaway. There are only eight individually furnished rooms decorated with a handpicked selection of Mexican handicrafts and delicate mosquito nets – and placed amidst calming colors and sober forms. The hotel design is a microcosm of Mexico's architectural legacy: clean lines, monochrome walls, and simple forms. Seen from the outside, it appears as a miniature terra-cotta palace. All in all, it is an ideal location for a refreshing stay away from all the hurly-burly.

Isla Mujeres – the Island of Women

Getting there and when to travel
Ferry: two possibilities: the passenger ferry in Juárez takes about 15 minutes and runs every ... from 6.30 to 22.30, and the car ferry from Punta Sa... departures daily.
Best travel time: bathing conditions all year around. ... rainy season in August and September.

Where to stay
****Casa de los Sueños*, Carretera a Garrafón, Lote 9. Tel: 998/877 06 51, fax: 887 07 08, www.casadelossuenos.com. This "dream house" with eight rooms located on Playa Indios is proud to offer individuality and tranquility. Zen and spa.

****Villa Rolandi Gourmet and Beach Club*, Laguna Mar L. 15. Tel: 998/877 07 00, fax: 887 01 00, www.villarolandi.com. Typical beach hotel. The good news: there are only twenty rooms and they are relatively large.
****Hotel Posada del Mar*, Av. Rueda Medina 15 A. Tel: 998/887 00 44, fax 887 02 66, e-mail: hotel@posadadelmar.com, offers good service at moderate prices and is situated close to North Beach and Playa Cocos. The 62 rooms are well ... and generously proportioned. Beautiful sea view from the restaurant.
**Elements of the Island*, Av. Benito Juárez 64. Tel: 998/977 07 36, e-mail: info@elementsoftheisland.co... Lisa from Austria and the Peruvian "Swiss" César rent three large rooms with cooking facilities in the town ce... just five minutes from the beach for $ 500 per week. G... Gózalo serves dark bread, cappuccinos and salads.

Must see
The Casa de Cultura, Av. Guerrero, offers workshops, a small library. Ecopark Garrafón, nature reserve with snorkeling and diving. Protective enclosure for sea turtles, Saco Bajo, open 9–17. Ix Chel temple and lighthouse on the southeastern tip of the island. Go up to the lighthouse platform for a great view of the surroundings. Delphin Discovery is situated in the southern part of the island for those who want to swim with dolphins: www.dolphindiscovery.com

Local Attractions
Two reclusive little islands to the north of Isla Mujeres: the bird reserve Isla Contoy by special permission only: www.islacontoy.org and the fishing island Holbox. Travel companies organize excursions to Isla Cozumel and to the Mayan Riviera: Xcaret and Xel Ha, also Tulum, Chichén Iztá, and Mérida.

Information
www.sedetur.qroo.gob.mx, www.gocancun.com, www.isla-mujeres.net

Traveling the Sisal Trail

Living the Life of a Lord of the Manor: Haciendas in

*Once upon a time, the sisal agaves brought wealth
Yucatán. The hemp plants that prosper under a Car
a synonym for Mexico. It's exciting to let oneself be
in time, set up base at a restored hacienda, and then set about
discovering Yucatán.*

It could be a shot from a film directed by the famous Sov
director Sergei Eisenstein: in the evening hours, when the hea
begins to let up and the sky is neither blue nor white, the aga
paint their shadows on the earth. Rising from a short, firm stem
their pointed leaves fan out, fleshy, sharp, and firm as lances. The
whole vista is an endless, geometric fugue in black and white of
row upon row of sisal agaves – the plant that made this region rich.
Traveling through northern Yucatán, visitors will find the "green
gold" of hemp plants everywhere. The agaves under the Mexican
sky are synonymous with Mexico.

This "most athletic of all plants," as it was once called by "roving
reporter" Egon Erwin Kisch, is really called henequén. But this name
seemed too awkward when it came to marketing the plant so it
was simply referred to as sisal – the name of the flourishing port
from which it was exported. Today, the port is little more than a
dot on the map. It silted up with time and traders began to use
the nearby port of Progreso. There are some beautiful beaches
close by but not a trace of the luxury that once held sway here.

All this happened some time ago. The sisal business stagnated after
the peak that it experienced during the two World Wars. The
development of synthetic fibers was the final death knell. At the
same time, world history was being acted out in Mexico. The first
revolution of the 20th century aimed at a just distribution of land.
"Tierra y libertad" – "Land and freedom" was the battle cry of
Emiliano Zapata and Pancho Villa. Under President Lázaro
Cárdenas, the Party of Institutionalized Revolution began to carry
out agricultural reforms in 1936: the end of the road for big
landowners, not all of whom had acquired their lands legally but
on the basis of bequests made at the time of the Spanish conquest

1 Mayan women drying sisal, Yucatán's green gold, at the Hacienda Santa
Rosa.
2 Secret star of the Hacienda Temozón.
3 A cenote near Dzinup on the Yucatán peninsular.
4 Past times on the Hacienda Temozón.

1 Classic case of luxury: swimming pool at the Hacienda Temozón.
2 "Traditional" lunchtime dining on the loggia at the Hacienda
Temozón …
3 … and romantic evening meals at the Hacienda Rosa.
4 and 5 The furnishings will take you back to another time.

that time had turned into fact. The plantation owners made the indigenous population toil like slaves on their fields.

Today, there is a market for natural products once again. Sisal is up and coming – as are the haciendas, but in a new context. The country mansions of the landed gentry so long neglected and allowed to fall to rack and ruin have been restored and turned into splendid hotels. One of the movers and shakers in this renewal is Mexico's star architect, Salvador Reyes Rios, who put his stylistic stamp on two very different haciendas: Petac, conserved in the Andalusian-Moorish style, and San José in Cacalchen, in which he reintroduced and reinterpreted the Mayan traditions.

It is a very special experience to overnight in one of these haciendas before setting off to explore the sights of Yucatán, a little like traveling back through time. We chose the Hacienda Santa Rosa de Lima. It is situated near Becal on the road between Campeche and Mérida, where it was one of the first to be founded in the region. Initially, its business was horse breeding and corn farming but about 100 years ago it switched to sisal. The machine room with the desfibradora, the defibering machine, still exists. That aside, however, the luxurious hotel with its open arcades dazzles its guests with Mexico's most beautiful colors: sunflower yellow, carmine red, and sapphire blue. Six junior suites with their own pool and Mayan huts-cum-bathrooms lie scattered in the

sprawling grounds. One cistern was turned into a swimming pool. Meals are taken outside on spacious terraces.

The Hacienda Temozón and its rambling park are situated close to Uxmal. It was once the biggest sisal plantation in the country and belonged to the governor of Yucatán so its size comes as no surprise. The comfort and design of the estate, bathed in royal burgundy red, is also gigantic: the pool could easily host water polo tournaments. Bougainvilleas cascade down house walls. The interior furbishing evokes the heyday of hacienda hospitality just as impressively: like the former plantation owners, the guests now relax on furniture from the Belle Époque.

How about a little history after all this space and luxury? Route 261 from Mérida to Uxmal takes us to the Hacienda Yaxcopoil. Its owners are descended from a Bavarian family. The grand estate with its representative entrance – an ornamental Moorish double arch under whispering palms – dates back to the 17th century and now houses a museum. In the old days, the estate comprised 22,000 hectares of land, but today the sisal agaves appear only in an ornamental context: the rooms, salons, and terraces showcase furniture from past epochs. Mirrors, candelabras, and crystal have been imported from Europe. A special room is devoted to finds from the Mayan era.

Haciendas in Yucatán – traveling the sisal trail

Getting there and when to travel
Air: the airport serving Yucatán province is Mérida. Daily flights from Acapulco, Mexico City, Cancún, and Oaxaca. Some connections also available via Campeche and Cancún.
Car: Rent a car if you want to take your time. Rental services available at the airports of Mérida, Campeche and Cancún. Reservations are best made in advance.
Best travel time: rainy season from August to October, agreeably cool in the winter months.

Where to stay
*****Hacienda Santa Rosa de Lima*. Tel: 999/944 36 37, fax: 944 84 84, eleven stylishly furnished rooms with stunning private terraces, a real resort with comprehensive service in a refined atmosphere. www.luxurycollection.com
****Hacienda Temozón, same contact details as above, vast grounds, a picture of an estate with particular attention to room furnishings.
*****Hacienda Petac, an unusual synthesis of Mexican colors, cool purism, and traditional hacienda style. The swimming pool was constructed within a former water cistern. The hacienda also offers cottage rentals. www.haciendapatec.com

Local Attractions
Museo Hacienda Yaxcopoil: located directly on the Mérida-Uxmal road. A working hacienda until 1984, the museum now showcases old furniture in the former living quarters as well as a desfibradora (defibering machine) in the machine room that was in use until 1913. The hacienda had its own school, its own hospital, and its own storeroom. A small guesthouse is available for overnight stays. Tel: 999/900 11 93, e-mail: hacienda@axcopoil.com
Dzibilchaltún: 23 km (14 miles) north of Mérida, a Mayan site of particular longevity (1500 BC–1500 AD), with a cenote (limestone sinkhole) over subterranean waterways, and the Templo de las Siete Muñecas.

Information
Mérida municipal authorities in the Teatro Peón Contreras, Calle 60/57, www.yucatan.gob.mx

Coconut-Farming Region Strikes it Rich
Cancún, the Riviera Maya, and Mysterious Temples

Cancún is also called "Mexico's Miami" – but that is only part of the picture. The "test-tube town" has its fair share of commercial shopping centers and hotels but the architecture and the atmosphere also represent the modern Mexico – against a backdrop that puts Miami in the shade.

Who would have thought, 40 years ago, that a neglected fishing and coconut-farming region with halfheartedly restored Mayan temples on the Caribbean coast in the remote state of Quintana Roo would morph into the country's biggest tourist magnet? In those days, Johnny Weissmüller and Lana Turner sunned themselves in Acapulco, the most spectacular jet-set destination on the Pacific coast. But the rapidly increasing number of guests soon proved too much for the limited resources of the paradisiacal bay. And besides, the jet set was keen to keep a distance to the curious fans – especially when it came to being observed indulging in vast quantities of margaritas in the hotel bar. So Cancún was created – on a first-generation computer. Three Mexican bank managers initiated the project complete with a prophetic name: in the Mayan language, "Cancún" means "pot of gold." For a while, they were the local laughing stock: there seemed little chance of making a profit so far off the beaten track. But the Cancún project, set on the east coast of the unkempt peninsular of Yucatán on a 22-kilometer-long (14 feet) promontory between lagoon and sea, grew slowly and steadily skywards. It seems that the critics had underestimated the unquenchable thirst for sun, sea, and good times that has since attracted millions of visitors.

The "pot of gold" delivered more, far more, than its name promised. Today, there are thousands of hotel beds available here, in a whole variety of settings: take your pick between Sleeping Beauty's Castle, reed-covered boats, Moroccan kasbahs, pyramids or simple cement blocks. Cancún attracts Americans, above all, young Americans under 21. Here, they can taste the fruits that are forbidden at home: drinking and smoking and dancing the night away in endless parties. Low prices and quick and easy accessibility

1 Kukulkán Pyramid, Chichén Itzá.
2 A mariachi band on the beach.
3 Playa Delfines in Cancún's hotel zone.
4 Mayan palaces and pyramids look proudly out over the sea: simply stunning.

by air from Miami provide added incentives. But many tourists want more than just a cheap place to stay. For those in search of more individual charms, the melodiously named Riviera Maya extends about 100 kilometers (62 miles) to the south, past the towns of Playa del Carmen, Akumal, and Tulum to Punta Allen. Mayan settlers once made their home here – leaving behind splendid traces of their civilization in Tulum, Cobá, and Chichén Iztá. All three settlements can easily be visited from the holiday resorts on the Riviera Maya – Tulum itself is actually situated on the coast. There are numerous opportunities for excursions including unusual diving spots and the large nature reserve Sian Kaan. And attractions such as the mysterious cenotes, sinkholes over subterranean waterways that were once believed to have been used for the ritual drowning of Mayan virgins, add to the area's luster.

The huge increase in tourism has brought changes to the coastal region. The tiny and rather idyllic Playa del Carmen once featured a single main street: exotic dining was available only in the Las Máscaras Pizzeria whilst margaritas were mixed at the Blue Parrot bar. Today, the culinary choices are overwhelming. The backpack tourists that used to haggle over prices in Posada Lily or the stable-like Cabañas La Ruina are long since a thing of the past. Smaller tourist centers such as Playa Paraiso and Playa Secreto have grown up to the north and south. Hurricane Gilbert, which whirled over the Yucatán peninsular in 1988 and uprooted the palm trees, left destruction in its wake but also encouraged a new construction boom on the dream beaches of the Caribbean.

Another new development is Punta Maroma, an exclusive and well-hidden hotel, with which readers of the glossy "Condé Nast Traveler" are more likely to be familiar than the locals. Paamul, situated to the south of Playa del Carmen, caters to tourists with a more moderate budget and less interest in international flair. The name given to neighboring Puerto Aventuras says it all: no self-respecting local mackerel fisher would ever hit upon the idea of calling his village "adventure port." It is, in fact, a yacht harbor, with hotels and holiday apartments. Akumal, too, is not an old settlement with traditional structures but a large-scale tourism

1 Crystal-clear water in the park at Xcaret near Playa del Carmen.
2 Cancún's hotel zone, a drawing-board production.
3 Hotel palaces on the beach at Cancún.
4 They take life a bit more slowly to the south in Playa del Carmen.
5 More rough and ready: pier and beach in Puerto Morelos in the north, just before the Riviera Maya starts.

Developers in the Riviera Maya also have cast covetous eyes on the area to the south of Tulum. Although Punta Allen is the end of the road for the time being, the creators of Cancún, for whom the resort had developed too much of a proletarian flair, had plans to develop Sian Kaan to the south of Punta Allen into a luxury playground for travel millionaires weary of Cancún's overexposed charms. But Sian Kaan was declared a biosphere reserve by UNESCO in 1987 and the development plans were fortunately jettisoned in 2004. As our travel guide from Xcaret, who told us this story, would say: "Too bad! ... Back to the computer." The locals are not at all happy with the idea that a biosphere reserve would simply be sold to the highest bidder for exclusive exploitation rights.

project set in one of the area's best diving bays. Tulum, on the other hand, dazzles visitors not only with its beaches of gleaming white sand but also with its picturesque Mayan ruins.

In Xcaret we find crystal-clear water – which the sun has turned into a glittering, green mirror. We dive down between water lilies and immerse ourselves in the magical atmosphere. Although Xcaret resembles a huge, flashy, American theme park in which you can spend a whole day doing all kinds of things, it has also retained its quietly impressive aspects. A little further to the south there is another opportunity to see a place dominated by an artificial, service-oriented atmosphere turn into a spot of enchanted nature: the nature park Xel Ha has several water pools, a large, curved, bay and the river Xel Ha itself with two cenotes that await visitors after a refreshing swim between the colorfully striped and glittering fishes.

Cenotes are the holy springs devoted to the Mayan god of rain, Chaac. They develop when underground waterways undermine the limestone strata above them until these collapse. They exude a mysterious magic and are full of clear water that slowly flows through the deep blue recesses. Divers have found gold and jade

in their depths – as well as human bones, which indicate sacrificial rites. Geologists say that a massive meteor crashed here millions of years ago and created the network system of cenotes that runs through the entire peninsular. Divers from all over the world come here today to explore the underground labyrinth of caves and canals that lead off from the cenotes. Waterways played a major role as transport channels during the Mayan era when this area was an important trade center. Major religious sites were also located here: Palenque was already deserted by the time this region developed between 1000 and 1500 AD. Besides Tulum, constructed as a coastal fortification, Xaman Ha (Playa del Carmen), Xcaret, and Xel Ha were further junctions on which settlements developed. Cobá is situated inland and was built during the Classic Mayan era between 300 and 1000 AD. It boasted a sometime population of about 50,000 – making it the largest city of its time. The island of Cozumel served as a pilgrimage site in honor of the mother goddess Ix Chel. Chichén Iztá lies a little further inland in the heart of the Yucatán peninsular. Its well-preserved and restored temples are not exclusively Mayan but offer enough substance for anybody interested in acquainting themselves more closely with the world of the Maya.

When the Spanish caravels sailed through the Caribbean in 1518, Tulum was not yet inhabited. During the nights, lights flickered along the coast to provide the Mayan canoes with orientation points. Today, the former harbor town is the most enchanting archeological site on the peninsular. Turquoise-green waves caress the rocks below while the fortress, whitewashed with salty spray on deeply fissured rocks, sits enthroned amongst a few windswept

1 Characteristic of Chichén Itzá: the intermingling of Mayan and Toltec culture from Mexico's central highlands.
2 Players had to shoot a heavy India rubber ball from the hip straight through this stone ring during ball games.
3 The figure of the rain god Tlaloc in Chichén Itzá served as a sacrificial altar.
4 – 5 Going up the main temple in Cobá is not as difficult as coming down.

1 Hotel Paradisus Riviera Cancún near Puerto Morelos.
2 Wellness oasis in the Ceiba del Mar in Puerto Morelos.
3 Fantastic views over the Caribbean are a feature of every balcony in the Ceiba del Mar.
4 For romantics: footbridge to the pool in the Hotel Paradisus Riviera Cancún.

palm trees. The best part of the ruins: the stucco ornamentation on the façades. You will have to dampen your enthusiasm slightly when looking at the famous Templo de los Frescos since its frescoes can be viewed only from a safe distance because the barrage of camera flashes set of by earlier tourist generations resulted in severe fading. There are road connections to the recently discovered old Mayan city of Cobá from both Playa del Carmen and Tulum. The Nohoch Mul Pyramid measures 42 meters (138 feet) that have to be climbed on fairly steep steps – but the view from the top over dense bush forests is worth the effort. There is much excavation work still to be done here, hidden in a network of tree roots that seem unwilling to let modernity in. But it is still a great pleasure to wander along the wide, cobbled alleys – the scabés – and ponder on the age and beauty of all this history.

On March 21 and September 23, the spring and fall equinoxes, Chichén Iztá, the country's biggest archeological site, is home to a very special event. Thousands of pilgrims make their way in the fading evening light to the mighty pyramid of the god Kukulcan to observe the great figure of a serpent wind its way from the top of the pyramid to its base. Architects and astronomers pooled all their knowledge to create this effect and visitors maintain, even today, that the pyramid gives off a very special energy at this moment. For all those who cannot share this experience, a special light and sound installation recreates it every evening – only without that special spiritual feeling.

Chichén Iztá can be reached from Cancún, Tulum, and Cobá. Just by dint of its dimensions, it puts the other pyramid sites in the shade. The Itza people bestowed its name, meaning "at the mouth of the well of the water enchanter," in the 5th century AD. The magical figure of Quetzalcoátl, the exiled god-king of the powerful Tula people, turned up again in Yucatán, indicating an intermingling with cultural influences from the Mayan people who worshipped him as Kukulcan. Chichén Iztá, the city that dominated the entire peninsular during at the height of its power, fell into decline around 1200 AD.

The carefully restored temples and frescoes in Chichén Iztá are like an open history book. The number of steps in the Kukulcan temple total 365, the number of days in a sun year. The Caracol is famous for its interior stairway that winds its way up to the top into the cupola, where an observatory was situated. Legend has it that young girls were sacrificed in the cenote that is situated to the north of the settlement.

Whilst analyses have not confirmed this, it remains highly likely. Gruesome and mysterious details dominate the temple platforms: animals gorging on human hearts. "One Thousand Pillars" frame the Temple of the Warriors; they are stele, covered with relief plaques showing warriors in full armor. The god of rain, Chaac, is also an important deity.

The accommodation opportunities are as varied as the coast itself. A whole new world opens up when you set foot in Ceiba del Mar, a luxury resort with 120 rooms situated directly on the beach of Puerto Morelos. Guests can relax here far from the party crowds and spoil themselves on 800 square meters of wellness oasis. Those with a more rustic taste should try the cheerfully colorful Cabañas Ana y José in Tulum.

Cancún – Coconut-farming region strikes it rich

Getting there and when to travel
Air: good connections to the international airport at Cancún, also served by charter airlines. Further regional airports in Mérida and Chetumal.
Bus: Cancún is the local bus junction. Frequent service along the Riviera Maya and to Mérida and Chetumal.
Best travel time: all year. Storms may occur in August and September.

Where to stay
*****Ceiba del Mar*, Costera Norte, Lote 01, Puerto Morelos. Tel: 998/872 80 60, www.ceibadelmar.com. Luxury, tranquility, and relaxation. Restrained evocation of local architecture: wood, whitewashed bungalows, palm roofs, spa area.
****El Deseo*, 5a Avenida and Calle 12, Playa del Carmen. Tel: 984/879 36 20, www.hoteldeseo.com, smart, new, designer hotel in purist style.
***Hotel Colibri*, attractive beach hostel in Playa del Carmen with pretty garden, www.hotel-colibri.com

****Cabañas Ana y José*, Carretera Tulum Bocapaila, km 7. Tel: 998/887 54 70, fax: 887 54 69, www.anayjose.com, right on the beach, not in the town: rustic, comfortable, spacious bungalows. Restaurant serves food cooked with typically Mayan herbs. Spa area and Temazcal.
***Posada del Sol*, Carretera Tulum-Punta Allen. Tel: 984/876 62 06, e-mail: laposada-delsol@hotmail.com, a friendly, new hostel for smaller budgets.

Must See
Holiday park Xcaret, 10 km (6 miles) to the south of Playa del Carmen, is an ideal destination for snorkeling, diving, swimming, sometimes in underground rivers: show programs also performed. Recommended: the Lagune Xel Ha to the south of Akumal.

Local Attractions
Isla Mujeres via ferry from Puerto Juárez, relatively peaceful diving and snorkeling region, most hotels situated in the northwest. Cozumel is busier and has more shopping opportunities, accessible by ferry from Playa del Carmen and Puerto Morelos (car ferry). Good diving and snorkeling here as well.
Sian Kaan biosphere reserve situated on the coast, Mexico's largest nature reserve with lagoon landscape. Apply to Amigos de Sian Kaan. Tel: 998/884 95 83 for excursions and hotels.

Information
www.rivieramaya.com, www.quintanaroo.gob.mx
Cancún Convention and Visitor Center. Tel: 981/884 65 31, www.gocancun.com

Mayan Magic
Palenque – City in the Jungle

Palenque promises fascinating insights into the mysterious history of Mayan culture. The palace and temple ruins that nestle in the verdant jungle of Chiapas continue to testify to the progressive construction methods employed by the Maya and to the beauty of their architecture.

Droplets of water gather in the tree tops of the tropical forest, the dark earth seems to steam in the mist. Orchids and frangipani flowers glow in the undergrowth. Squawking parrots drown out the sound of the crickets. Howling monkeys bawl through the jungle. We have reached a high terrace in the middle of a low-lying area, surrounded by small waterfalls that tumble through the River Otulúm. Myriads of small, yellow butterflies and shimmering dragonflies flutter around the wanderer; the cobalt blue morpho butterfly disappears into the shadowy forest. This natural treasure trove is an absolutely fitting setting for what we are about to see: one of the most enchanting archeological fields in the world, the garden city and ceremonial center of the Maya in Palenque.

The site preserved today was founded in 642 AD and deserted around 950: to this day, nobody knows exactly why. Latest research indicates that this city, home to the Mayan nobility, had to submit to attacks by an inimical Mayan regent from Calakmul. Prisoners were not taken in those days. Warriors were doomed to a sacrificial death, announced with tuneful melodies played on conch shell trumpets.

The Mayan name for Palenque was Lakam Ha – "big water." It was the capital of B'aakal, one of the most important and wealthiest city-states of the 40 to 50 Mayan principalities in the tropical lowlands, and comprised about 6 square kilometers (2.3 square miles) of cleared land on which 10,000 to 15,000 people lived. In contrast to European cities of the same era that often served as trade junctions, Lakam Ha served purely religious and ceremonious functions. The settlement was ruled by Chul Ajaws, the holy kings. The most famous Mayan regent in Palenque was called Janaab Pakal: his palace and the burial chamber known as the "House of

1–4 The Mayan city of Palenque in the tropical rainforest of Chiapas is one of the most fascinating collection of ruins in southeastern Mexico. Important tomb treasures from the time of King Pacal were found here, most recently in 1994 immediately next to the Temple of Inscriptions.

1 Temple in the ruined city of Bonampak in the region populated by the Lacandon Maya. Frescoes depicting scenes from Mayan social life were found in the temple chambers in 1946 by Charles Frey, an American photographer and adventurer.
2 The Gubernatorial Palace in Palenque.
3–4 Temple in Palenque.
5 The Yajip waterfalls near Bonampak.

the Nine Figures" have been reconstructed and are situated on the southern edge of the hill. So far, only a small portion of the buildings has been uncovered – 34 out of an estimated 500 buildings – of which only a dozen have been restored. But such as they are, the pyramids of up to 65 meters (204 feet) in height, the palaces and temples with their steep stairs, terraces, and their splendid roof ridges, or cresterías, all serve to create an impression of great solemnity and grace. Today, the buildings have weathered to a kind of whitish-gray limestone but they originally shone in a warm vermilion red. The faces of the gods and their symbols were also painted in different colors.

About 500 years after the Maya had left Lakam Ha, serious and systematic research began to unravel the secrets of their city-state. Interest had been sparked by a report written by the North

American travel writer and archeologist John L. Stephens, published in 1841 with illustrations by Frederick Catherwood: "Here was the legacy of a cultivated and refined nation ... in the midst of all the destruction, we saw the dark forest begin to

recede and we began mentally to restore each of the buildings to its original and undamaged condition, to reconstruct the sculptures and drawings … We tried to imagine how those sad figures that looked down upon us now from high up on the walls must have appeared when they were alive, ascending the palace terraces or temple steps in imaginatively designed garments and feathered plumes. It must have been a fabulous scene of unique beauty …"

Sixty years after its discovery by a Spanish priest, Stephens' fanatical curiosity made sure that the ruined Mayan city became known to a wide public. In 1923, the Danish architect Frans Blom began to excavate.

The Classic Mayan period notched up a huge number of scientific achievements. Although they were not aware of the wheel or capable of metal foundry, they were able to come to precise conclusions concerning the stars and the nature of the universe. Several calendars were developed; the Maya calculated the exact duration of a sun year and the length of a moon phase, knew that Venus revolved around the sun, and were able to work out the dates of sun and moon eclipses.

Today, we know that the Maya developed complicated irrigation systems to drain the low-lying swamps. They relied primarily on corn for subsistence but also cultivated chilies, avocados, nuts, guavas, sweet potatoes, cassavas, cucumbers, and squash, as well as several herbs.

Illustrations and frescoes uncovered on this site and many others tell us that the Maya were very image conscious and submitted to painful operations in order to measure up to contemporary beauty standards: babies' heads were squashed so that they would take on the much admired length of face with receding foreheads, teeth were filed to a sharp point and enamel was removed so that jade splinters could be inserted for decorative purposes, both women and men were tattooed. The properties of tobacco were known and appreciated – not least for medicinal purposes. Copal was used as incense and a delicious drink was mixed using cocoa beans and water – what we call chocolate today. Their world was filled with magic – nothing was without a soul. Priest-kings had unlimited powers. They alone were allowed to enter the holy of holies on the uppermost platforms. The vertiginous ascent of the steps symbolized the distance between the common man and the sacrosanct ruler.

Back now to Lakam Ha: one of the first buildings we see after entering is the labyrinthine palace begun under Pakal (626–683) and extended by his successors to encompass nine further walkways, rooms, and courtyards. It is a splendid building with many stairs, entrances, corridors, and chambers, surmounted by a tall, well-built tower that could have been either an observatory or a watchtower. Only fragments of the ornamentation, stucco elements, paintings, and stele remain today – partly the fault of early archeologists who simply burnt down the jungle to get at the hidden temples and palaces.

The "House of Nine Figures," also called Temple of Inscriptions, is situated to the west of the palace. This is where a team of excavators under Ruz l'Huillier discovered Palenque's most spectacular treasure in 1952: the grave of the Maya King Pacal, buried in a kind of crypt under a burial slab that weighed eight tons. This slab is decorated with such a wonderful relief portrait that Pacal in all his stylized glory seems to rise before the visitors. The valuable tomb treasures with the King's famous jade mask are now on show in the Anthropological Museum in Mexico City. Glyph-slabs on the wall gave the tomb its name. The three temples to the west were dedicated to Pacal's son, Kan B'alum.

Archeologists have identified him on numerous relief engravings and paintings. The Temple of the Foliated Cross, the Temple of the Cross, and the Temple of the Sun are smaller and built to face each other. Each features three entrances, separated by pillars, the typical pointed or corbel arch (the "false" Mayan arch) and cresterías, the elaborately decorated, stone roof ridges. The figures on the pillars flanking the entrance to the Temple of the Cross show Kan B'alam himself and a priest.

The smaller Temple of the Jaguar lies hidden in the undergrowth, named for a stone slab that has now disappeared. It showed a Mayan prince riding on a jaguar. The remains of some living quarters were found on the hill behind the temple. A further pyramid was built near the palace and tomb of Pacal, believed to have been constructed as a tomb for Pacal's mother: the remains of a woman aged about 40, decorated with splendid jade jewelry, were found in the burial chamber.

Many of the pyramids and buildings in Lakam Ha have not been identified; many secrets still slumber among the temple stones, under the jungle's protective canopy.

We chose the Chan Kah resort village as the point of departure for our visits to Palenque. It has something of the magic of the

Palenque – the Magic of the Maya

Getting there and when to travel
Air: the nearest airports are Mérida and Campeche.
Bus: service to Villahermosa, Campeche, and San Cristóbal de las Casas. Minibus and estate car service to the entrance of the archeological sites, about 8 km (5 miles).
Best travel time: all year. No great changes in weather conditions. Rainy season between May and September.

Where to stay
****Chan Kah resort*, Carretera Ruinas. Tel: 916/345 11 34, www.chan-kah.com, a well-planned bungalow resort in which to relax after visiting Palenque. Nice pool and beautiful gardens. Situated outside the town of Palenque.

****Misión Palenque*, Rancho San Martín de Porris. Tel: 916/345 02 41, www.hotelesmision.com, large two-storey house with its own thermal spa, swimming pool and garden.

***Hotel Nututún*, Carretera Palenque – Ocosingo, km 3.5 (2 miles). Tel: 916/345 01 00, 345 06 33, www.nututun.com, pool, garden, camping site, playground, and small lake, also situated outside Palenque.

***Villas Kin-Ha*, situated about 2.5 km (1.5 miles) from the ruins. 90 small, well-kept rooms in several bungalows, comfortable suites. Swimming pool.

Must See
The Museo del Sitio in Palenque shows a reconstruction of Pacal's tomb and the most recent findings taken from temples XIX, XX, XXI, stucco relief work and a throne fragment (open Tue–Sun, from 10–16).

Local Attractions
The Maya Express provides a luxurious means of transport to historically interesting sites on the peninsular. Several different itineraries that end in Mérida and Campeche; stops include Palenque, Edzná, Uxmal, museums and cenotes: special trip available to Chichén Itzá. www.expresomaya.com A new road and ferry connection over the Río Usumacinta will take you to the Maya ruins of Yaxchilán and Bonampak. The beautiful waterfalls of Agua Azul, good for swimming, are situated to the southwest of Palenque.

Information
www.mesoweb.com, website for fans of Mayan archeology.
Regional website: www.chiapas.gob.mex

1–2 Restaurant and bungalow in the Hotel Villas Kin-Há in Palenque.
3 Frescoes in Palenque.
4 Mayan figure in the Hotel Villas Kin-Há.

nearby Mayan city. The swimming pools and delicious cuisine ensure relaxation. A perfect holiday hotel – in the middle of the jungle.

Into the Heart of Indian Territory
San Cristóbal de las Casas and the Mayan Villages

No other colonial city in Mexico was so strongly influenced by Indian cultures as San Cristóbal de las Casas in the highlands of Chiapas. It is the cultural and religious syncretism embodied by the town's atmosphere that makes the town unique.

Wood-smoke aromas waft over the awakening city of San Cristóbal de las Casas. The morning mist streams out of dense oak and pine woods, settles over the roofs, dampens the old-fashioned cobbles on the streets. Nights can get pretty cold up here at an altitude of 2,100 meters (6,900 feet) above sea level.

The old colonial city of San Cristóbal des las Casas in the state of Chiapas was founded in 1528 by the Spanish conquistador Diego de Mazariegos. Based on the quality of its architecture, many regard it as Mexico's most beautiful city. The zócalo, set between arcaded façades, basks in its own harmony. Red-tiled roofs cast shadows over house walls that have been painted in light pastel shades, often carefully decorated with old-fashioned advertisements or political slogans. Doorjambs surrounded by red sandstone, windows protected by elaborate wrought-iron trellises; romanticism is a by-word here, permeating every corner of the poorer side streets with their crumbling stone walls.

The splendidly baroque Santa Domingo Church has altars and woodcarvings generously covered in gold plate. Every morning, the Mayan women of Zinacantán gather here, dressed in their raspberry pink and vanilla-colored capes. They are joined by the Mayan Tzotzil-Chamula women in black and dark blue with white blouses and those from Tenejapa, whose costumes are embroidered in bright red. They spread their arts and crafts products out for the customer: embroidery, warm shawls, woven tunics, and a particular favorite – the dolls with wool hats that were the trademark of the revolutionary Zapatista movement. They study us cautiously. Any attempt to take a photo of the picturesque scene is quickly rejected.

The arts and crafts cooperative Sna Jolobil has set up shop in the former monastery buildings. The "Association of Mayan Weavers from Chiapas" buys the products manufactured by village women

1 Jaguar in the zoo at Tuxtla Gutiérrez.
2 – 3 The Cathedral "Nuestra Senora de la Asunción" of San Cristóbal de las Casas.
4 The Chamula Indians only allow photographs once they have given their express permission. Contraventions are punishable.

and pays a good price. Their livelihoods are assured – and the metaphorical language inherent in their images lives on. The originals are on show in the adjacent Museo de los Altos de Chiapas.

The colonial, somewhat festive city charm is not the only attraction in San Cristóbal de las Casas. It is also the center, the home, and the research headquarters for a rich, Indian culture not easily viewed at such close quarters elsewhere in Mexico. The Tzotzil, Tzeltal, and Chamul Indians are heirs to age-old Mayan culture. They live close to San Cristóbal de las Casas, in villages that are situated at up to 3,000 meters (9,850 feet) above sea level. Life here would not be the same without them. The Swiss photographer Gertrude Duby and the Danish archeologist Frans Blom were the first to do extensive research in Palenque. In the 1940s, they "discovered" the hitherto hidden cosmos of the Lacandon Mayas. With their shoulder-length, gleaming black hair and their wide, white tunics, they seemed like messengers from a lost era, so very different from the colorful traditional costumes worn by their highland neighbors. The Spanish conquistadors

1 Santo Domingo Church in San Cristóbal de las Casas.
2 View over San Cristóbal.
3 Guacamaya parrot in Southern Mexico.
4 Typical market stall in San Cristóbal.
5 Tzotzil family in San Juan Chamula.

insisted on their wearing different kinds of dress – so as to be able to tell them apart (as malicious tongues would have it). "Na Bolom," the House of the Jaguar in which Blom and Duby lived on the Avenida Vicente Guerrero 33, now enjoys cult status. Frans and "Trudi" Blom are no longer alive, but their presence can be felt everywhere in the colonial house. Vivid black-and-white photos tell the story of the Lacandons, which some insist had better been left in the dark … but respect and great admiration remain for the archeologist and his wife.

Samuel Ruiz cannot be sure of such a warm reception. The charismatic former Bishop of San Cristóbal de las Casas mediated between the ZNLA, the Zapatista National Liberation Army, and the government of the day with the same degree of commitment and verve that he also displayed on behalf of the civil war refugees

from Guatemala and in translating the Bible into Indian languages. The spoiled child of wealthy, intellectual parents was determined to forge a career for himself in the Vatican but was given a posting in deepest Chiapas. It changed his outlook on life: the bitter poverty and profound religiosity of the Indian population turned him into a burning advocate for their world – even if it contradicted everything he believed in as a Catholic. Maybe San Cristóbal de las Casas is the right place to examine one's own special view of the world inhabited by the indígenas? It has long been an important stop for those interested in ethnology and committed to social welfare, providing, as it does, an excellent starting point for visiting the surrounding Indian communities and studying their particularly authentic Indian lifestyle. And the Café Galería in the Calle Hidalgo 5 has long been a place for students of these issues who have come from far-flung places to meet and get down to some serious discussion. We climb up the street that leads from the zócalo to the second-class bus terminal, the point of departure for the brightly painted vehicles that do the rounds of the surrounding villages. The smell of corn that accompanies

every trip in Mexico mingles with the wood smoke. Corn has been basic Mexican subsistence food since pre-Columbian times and is served in a variety of ways – including a specially brewed beer. The bus terminal is a good selling place for travelers who want to assuage their hunger before starting out. The cooks offer fresh corn tortillas served with chicken, tomatoes, coriander, and white cheese. It tastes simply delicious. A colorful market surrounds the bays from which the buses depart. The eye feasts on pyramids of gleaming tomatoes, piles of garlic and onions, on small, sweet, dark squash, and bundles of herbs spread out on reams of fabric. Pieces of white limestone are also on sale: a prerequisite for preparing tortillas.

One of the most fascinating destinations amongst the villages is San Juan Chamula, 11 kilometers (7 miles) away. It is the ceremonial center for the Chamula Tzotzil Indians – the place in which their rites are practiced most conspicuously: a Mayan Jesus was crucified here just 150 years ago in an attempt to create an alternative to the savior worshipped by the Spanish Catholic clergy. The grand dame of Mexican literature, Rosario Castellanos, wrote a book on the death of this child entitled The Book of Lamentations. The Chamula revere sheep as sacred animals and bury them in a special site. The village is situated between wooded hollows and is grouped around a whitewashed church. It is decorated with

colorful flower friezes and looks out over a large square that quickly fills with procession participants on religious holidays. Pale light filters into the church. The floor is covered with fresh pine needles. Ritual drinking sessions are held here amid the scent of burning copal, and the figures of saints that line the walls are quickly divested of their glass coverings if they fail to deliver the desired miracles. Any participant is welcome to attend the religious festivals, but photography is forbidden in the church and only allowed outside with the express permission of the subject – and after suitable remuneration. Only men take part in the processions. Later, we visit Tenejapa, where we feel slightly less out of place. San Ildefonso Church is a prime example of cultural heritage but more famous yet are the local women, renowned for their weaving and embroidery skills. Local lore has gone so far as to explain their dexterity by attributing it to the presence of a Catholic saint, although it can safely be assumed that St Lucia would have frowned upon their motifs, which are definitely Indian and therefore also heathen. The Sunday market is famous throughout the region.

Teresa and Daniel Suter Rodríguez make you feel welcome in the Posada El Paraíso in San Cristóbal: their hospitality ensures a relaxed, communicative atmosphere. Tours and riding excursions are organized on request.

San Cristóbal de las Casas – into the Indian heartlands

Getting there and when to travel
Air: frequent service from Mexico City to the provincial capital of Chiapas, Tuxtla Gutiérrez. From there, it's a two-hour bus ride to San Cristóbal.
Bus: reservations are advisable. Connections to Comitán, Palenque, Mérida, Oaxaca, Mexico City, Tapachula, and Villahermosa. Connections to Agua Azul, Chiapa de Corzo, and the surrounding villages leave from the second-class terminal.
Best travel time: warmest from May to September. Cool night temperatures in the winter.

Where to stay
**Posada El Paraíso*, 5 de Febrero 19. Tel: 967/678 00 85, fax: 678 51 68. The Mexican-Swiss couple Teresa and Daniel Suter Rodríguez turned an empty 100-year-old hospital into a very cozy hotel with 14 rooms and intimate atmosphere. It is two blocks away from the Plaza. Riding excursions organized on request. Mountain bike rental.
**Casavieja*, María Adelina Flores 27. Tel. and fax: 976/678 68 68, www.casavieja.com.mx, an 18th-century colonial house transformed into a comfortable hotel.
**Na Bolom Guesthouse*, Av. Vicente Guerrero 33. Tel. and fax: 967/678 14 18, www.nabolom.org, part of the former living quarters inhabited by Frans Blom and Gertrude Duby. 15 differently furnished and decorated little suites, surrounded by a large garden. Archive, museum, excursions, cultural exchange programs.

Must See
Santo Domingo Monastery: home to the Museo de los Altos de Chiapas: regional history, arts and crafts cooperative Sna Jolobil. More arts and crafts at Ipas Joloviletek in the Gral. Utrilla 43; Photo exhibitions of the Lacandon Mayas in Real de Guadalupe Street, House of the Jaguar. Interesting food market run by indigenous Indians in the Gral. Utrilla/Nicaragua.

Local Attractions
Tzeltal and Tzotzil, Zinacantán, San Juan Chamula, and Tenejapa are all easy to reach by bus. The festivities in honor of San Juan on June 24 in San Juan Chamula are particularly impressive.

Information
The municipal authorities situated on the zócalo provide a tourist information service. www.chiapas.gob.mx

1 Pool in the Hotel Villas Kin-Hà near Palenque.
2 Typical for San Cristóbal: the rustic architecture of the Posada El Paraíso.
3 and 5 loggia and great dining table of the Paraíso.
4 Unique: the ethnological museum "Na Bolom," founded in 1951 by Frans Blom and Gertrude Duby-Blom houses 5,000 documents and 50,000 negatives.

Retracing the Steps of Hernán Cortés
Veracruz, La Antigua, and the Shamans of Catemaco

Happy – no better word to describe the atmosphere on the Plaza de Armas, Veracruz' zócalo. The town has an exciting history and is set in beautiful surroundings dotted with enchanting towns and villages.

Shining arcades surround the zócalo of Veracruz. Sounds of melodious harps and the marimbas that resonate under the rhythmic touch of the mallets drift through the air. Today, as every day, musicians and bands have come to the Plaza de Armas to play traditional tunes or local versions of North American hits on the marimba. The wooden instrument – a cousin of the xylophone, around which up to four players may gather although it is normally just two – has an infectiously rousing sound. It is generally accompanied by rattles and a guitar. Legend has it that "La Bamba" originated in Veracruz and if you've ever heard that swinging tune, you'll know what Veracruz sounds like. Its city center seems to swing along, especially during carnival, when the whole place turns into a stage for ten days and the entire harbor promenade is transformed into a dance floor for hot samba rhythms.

We are here on a " normal" weekday and are drinking what is rumored to be the best coffee in the world in the Café de la Parroquia, under the arcades. It's just a few steps to the Plaza de Armas, the city's hub and nerve center.

A new promenade that starts at the harbor winds its way along the coastline for miles to Boca del Río. The former fishing village situated on the estuary of the Jamapa River has been transformed into a modern and chic suburb that houses luxury hotels, restaurants, shopping centers, and discos. But we prefer to return to the zócalo. You could spend days here, keeping out of the sun under the arcades, listening and looking and indulging in an habanero (grape schnapps mixed with sugar cane), or a jobo (a wine made from fermented grapes) in the evening. Earlier, we might have eaten some of the delicious shrimps, camarones enchipotlados, in one of the typical one-room restaurants down by the harbor, or maybe the huachinango veracruzana, perch

1 Spring on the Gulf of Mexico.
2 Fishers ...
3 ... and storks on Lake Catemaco.
4 The Faro Venustiano Carranza lighthouse in the morning mist typical of Veracruz. In 1915, during the revolution, it served as residence to interim President Venustiano Carranza.

1 Parish Church of Catemaco.
2 The cozy town of Santiago Tuxtla.
3 Typical for Tlacotalpan: the colorful façades with barred windows.
4 Real Jarrochos: street musicians in Boca del Rio in Veracruz.
5 Always cheerful: the romantic city of Tlacotalpan with its arcades.
6 Gleaming: formerly home to the municipal authorities of Boca del Rio; today, a smart Veracruz suburb.

cooked in a fruity, spiced tomato-caper-paprika sauce that is simply divine.

The city played an important role in Mexico's history. On Good Friday of the year 1519, the world order was reshuffled when Hernán Cortés first set foot on Mexican soil. The race against Portugal to appropriate overseas territories in the newly-discovered American subcontinent had started. Cortés christened the town Villa Rica de la Verdadera Cruz, or "Rich Town of the True Cross." He knew that the crews on the boats that had sailed with him across the ocean were not his most fervent supporters: in order to prevent opposition to the conquest, he had all the ships burned. Believing that Cortés was the reincarnation of the ruler Quetzacóatl, the Aztec emperor Moctezuma sent forth a delegation to welcome Cortés. But there was never any doubt

that Cortés had come to subjugate and exploit the newly-discovered country. From Veracruz, Cortés made his way over the mountains past Pico de Orizaba, Mexico's highest mountain, via Puebla and Tlaxcala towards Tenochtitlán, the center of Aztec rule.

Some Indian peoples joined forces with the Spaniard with the aim of toppling the powerful Aztec lord – for how else could Cortés have triumphed over Moctezuma and his warriors?

Until late in the last century, the artificial harbor constructed here by the Spaniards was Mexico's only embarkation port for Europe. Attracted by the colony's riches, pirates attacked Veracruz again and again until the Spaniards began to build the San Juan de Ulúa fortress in 1535. This is where the Spaniards fought to the death defending their privileges in the War of Independence before finally giving up in 1825. Two decades later, Veracruz was occupied by troops from north of the border in the Mexican-American War, and again by French troops two decades after that. The last attack on the city took place less than 100 years ago, when the Americans attempted to stop the revolution and occupied the city for several months. The restored San Juan de Ulúa fortress is now a museum – comprising the former cell of Mexican President and first Zapotec to occupy this office, Benito Juárez (1858–1861). The Faro Venustiano Carranza lighthouse situated a few steps away is where Venustiano Carranza, interim president during the Mexican revolution, lived in 1915. Today, it is a national memorial.

The so-called Ruta de Cortés begins in Veracruz by following a well-built coastal road to La Antigua – which maintains that it marks the site of the original Veracruz. It was here, so they say in La Antigua, and not in contemporary Veracruz, that Cortés first stepped onto Mexican soil. And here, so they continue, was the site of the first Mexican church. Who knows today which version is true? On the other hand, why shouldn't the Casa de Cortés – the ruined house girdled by massive tree roots in La Antigua, 15 kilometers (9 miles) from the town of Veracruz – be the house in which the conquistador lived? There is something appealing about the way the locals have left this house to decay: not honored, not restored, not glorified.

In Zempoala we return to Indian history. This archeological site, situated just north of La Antigua, used to be the capital of the Totonacs, one of the Indian peoples that supported the bearded strangers on their way north towards Tenochtitlán. The ceremonial area that dates back to this era has survived, spread out over several platforms. The Palacio Las Chimeneas rises on its eastern edge – the Templo Mayor of the Totonac kings. It is called the "Chimney Palace" because of its many hollow pillars and niches.

Our route continues towards the southeast. Just after Boca del Rio, the country road takes us into one of Mexico's loveliest landscapes, the Los Tuxtlas region with Lake Catemaco and the picturesque town of Tlacotalpan, situated on the estuary of the River Papaloapan. The dainty little town of San Andrés Tuxtla is famous for the tobacco that is grown here and harvested for the manufacture of cigars that can easily hold a candle to those from Cuba. Tlacotalpan's marvelous colonial architecture has added it to the list of UNESCO World Heritage Sites. It is characterized by shaded arcades and colorful façades, whose big windows are hidden behind mighty iron railings and their abundantly planted patios. The treasures of the former colonial lords are still on show in some of the mansions: pianos, select furniture, valuable porcelain, and fabrics from Austria, Germany, and Spain.

1 Move over, Cohiba: Mexico's finest cigars come from San Andrés Tuxtla in Veracruz.
2 Dreams in linen: splendid but simple, a suite in the Hacienda Uayamón atmospherically located in the middle of the jungle. Further highlights are:
3 … the terrace …
4 … the pool in the former machine room, where workers once toiled
5 as well as the restaurant.

Catemaco, situated on the eponymous lake, is unique. Nestled in between gentle hills and green pastures, it bears a certain resemblance to Lake Constance. Catemaco is a center for shamans, magicians, and wizards. Once a year they come here from all four corners of the world to attend the Congress of Witchcraft Practitioners. There are potions and spells here for every condition – sickness, love-sickness, financial indigence: whatever your plight, a visit to the island of Nancyaga in the middle of the lake will provide an answer. Take the speedboat to the privately-run ecological and amusement park. If you want to entertain your fellow visitors, why not apply a face mask consisting of mud from the lake bottom – or have a shaman cleanse your body of "bad spirits" with a "limpia," consisting of aromatic smoke, a bunch of exotic smelling herbs, some splashes of blessed water, and some incomprehensible incantations. When all is said and done – and paid – he'll give you an amulet and dismiss you from his hut. On the way back, the boat passes by a small island populated solely by monkeys imported from Thailand to entertain the tourists with their chatter. The regional fish dishes served in the lakeside restaurants are a revelation.

Veracruz – retracing the steps of Hernán Cortés

Getting there and when to travel
Air: Aeroméxico, Mexicana and Aeromar as well as Delta Airlines fly to Veracruz.
Bus: hourly bus service between Mexico City, Jalapa and Veracruz. Bus terminal in Jalapa: Av. 20 de Noviembre; in Veracruz: Av. Salvador Díaz Mirón 1698. Bus tickets also sold in shopping centers.
Best travel time: from September to June. Very humid and warm during central European summer months. The "Nortes," low-pressure troughs, are known for their sudden onslaught of cold air.

Where to stay
*****Hotel Emporio*, Insurgentes Veracruzanos. Tel: 229/932 00 20, fax: 931 22 51, www.hotelesemporio.com, modern, light, spacious, and elegant hotel with large rooms, three pools, not far from the zócalo.
***Hotel Colonial Posada*, situated directly on the Plaza de Armas (zócalo). Tel: 229/932 01 93; restored colonial-style house. Rooms to the back are quiet.

***Posada Doña Lala*, center of Tlacotalpan. Tel: 288/884 25 80, fax: 884 24 55, e-mail: Posada_lala@hotmail.com, comfortable rooms on the river near the Plaza.

Must See
The Carnival in Veracruz is the most famous South American carnival after Rio.
Fiesta de la Candelaria, in Tlacotalpan, always in January.
Congress of Witchcraft Practitioners in Catemaco, always on the first Friday in March.

Local Attractions
Bathing resort Chachalacas to the north of La Antigua in the direction of Poza Rica, about one hour from Veracruz.
The Costa Esmeralda has nearly 50 km (31 miles) of paradisiacal beaches between Tecolutla and Nautla heading northwards. Some lovely hotels have been built here in the last few years.
El Tajín: the famous Pyramid of the Niches near Papantla, symbol of the Totonac culture about three and a half hours north of Veracruz. Home to the famous ceremony of "Papantla Flyers" (Voladores de Papantla).
Tres Zapotes: Pyramid site of the Olmecs near Santiago Tuxtla, about one hour south of Veracruz.

Information
Oficina de Convenciones y Visitantes del Estado de Veracruz, Blvd. Adolfo Ruiz Cortines No. 3497 (World Trade Center), Boca del Rio. Tel: 229/923 03 91, e-mail: ovc@vera-cruzovc.com.mx, www.veracruzturismo.com

On the Road in the Land of Milk and Honey
Jalapa, Xico and Coatepec

The land of milk and honey begins just after the rather less welcoming municipality of El Perote. Dense forests and luscious pastures spread into the distance as we pass by coffee, mango, banana, and sugar cane plantations. Suddenly, Jalapa lies before us, the capital of Veracruz state.

The university town of Xalapa (also called Jalapa), dotted around a hilly landscape, retains a slightly sleepy atmosphere – despite all efforts to appear busy and bustling. Lets take a walk over the three terraces in the Parque Juárez, a garden-like zócalo, that is framed, here as almost everywhere else in Mexico, by a cathedral, the Palacio Muncipal, and the Palacio de Gobierno. Steep alleys take us to the colorful market halls. The curbstones are impressively high – a reminder that heavy rainfall can turn the streets into rivers. Veracruz has an altitude of about 1,400 meters (4,600 feet), guaranteeing a mild climate but also generous amounts of precipitation and much fog.

The indigenous cultures that the Spanish extinguished and tried to replace with their own are still alive in Jalapa's main attraction: the Museo de Antropología, considered to be on a par with that in Mexico City. Over 3,000 years of Indian cultural life along the Gulf Coast are documented here in spacious, light-flooded rooms, worthily represented by the Olmec monumental sculptures in the museum garden, by the nearly life-size, hollow, clay figures by the Huastec of El Zapotal, and by the valuable jade jewelry. Many exhibition pieces come from the Tontac Palace of Niches in El Tajín near Papantla.

Situated only 120 kilometers (74 miles) from Veracruz and 300 kilometers (186 miles) from Mexico City, Xalapa was one of Mexico's most important stagecoach stations during the colonial era. The high standard of living enjoyed by the colonial masters is evident in houses such as the Hacienda El Lencero, which has been restored and furnished with period pieces. It is situated about 10 kilometers (6 miles) south of Xalapa, not far from the road to Veracruz, and was built by a fellow member of Hernán Cortés' army. The "house" (although this is something of an understatement) of an infamous

1 Fortín de las Flores in Veracruz: view over the Pico de Orizaba vulcano.
2 Totonacs in Papantla.
3 Monumental Olmec head in the archeological museum park in Xalapa near Veracruz.
4 Fantastic panorama near Fortín de las Flores with the Pico de Orizaba.

former general and President of Mexico is just as fascinating. Santa Ana was a central figure in the Mexican-American War and the house is worth visiting just for a glimpse into the man's personality. The spectacular view is an additional bonus.

Attracted by the fertile soil and the wonderful landscape, German emigrants settled here and began planting coffee. Legend has it that those emigrants who saw the Pico de Orizaba from the boat, long before they sailed into the harbor at Veracruz, were determined to make their new home here. There must have been quite a few of them. Country houses with a German name and a distinct resemblance to a Swiss chalet are liable to crop up suddenly in the landscape. The coffee farmers and the tourist association have come up with the idea of initiating a Ruta del Café: those interested in the coffee bean can visit plantations and learn about the production process.

The picturesque little city of Coatepec is synonymous with coffee and its products. The aroma of roasted coffee drifts out of the roasting houses, and the coffee liqueur Kahlúa and other delicious liqueurs made from guavas and peaches are produced here. Coatepec was an important agricultural center as early as the 18th

1 Real men: riders in Tlacotalpan, Veracruz.
2 The Texolo waterfall in the coffee-growing area near Xico in Veracruz state is a popular destination with abseiling enthusiasts.
3–4 The Hotel Posado Coatapec in Coatapec.
5 Figure in the Archeological Museum in Xalapa, Veracruz.

century, when citrus fruits, tobacco, and sugar cane were farmed here.

The lovely town of Xico, situated about 11 kilometers (9 miles) from Xalapa and southeast of Coatapec, provides visitors with a taste of what eco- and adventure tourists come here to enjoy. Xico marks the entrance to a fanstastic mountain landscape with imposing gorges and waterfalls as well as abundant flora and fauna – a dream destination for bikers, mountaineers, kayak and river rafting enthusiasts.

The trip on the curvy highway from Xalapa via Orizaba to Córdoba is breathtakingly beautiful – if it just happens to be a clear, fog-free day. Both Orizaba and Córdoba are colonial jewels. We let the day draw to a close sitting in a café under the arcades overlooking the zócalo.

Xalapa, Xico, Coatapec – traveling through the land of milk and honey

Getting there and when to travel
Air: Aeroméxico, Mexicana and Aeromar run flights to Xalapa from Mexico City.
Bus and car: there is no highway connection to Xalapa. Turning off from the Orizaba – Córdoba – Oaxaca highway just after Puebla near Tepeaca onto the busy long-distance transit road will take you to Xalapa via El Perote. There is a bus service from Mexico City (Central de Autobuses Lázaro Cárdenas) that runs every 30 minutes to Xalapa and Veracruz. Orizaba and Córdoba are directly connected by highway.
Best travel time: November to June. Very humid and warm during central European summer months. Frequent rainfall in Xalapa.

5

Where to stay
****Hotel Villa Las Margaritas Centro*, Dr. Rafael Lucio 186, Zentrum Xalapa. Tel: 01-228/815 06 11, fax: 840 08 86, e-mail: hvillam@hotmail.com, www.villasmargeritas.com
***Hotel Casa Inn Xalapa*, comfortable hotel with Mexican flair. Lovely view over the town and the Pico de Orizaba. Av. 20. de Noviembre 522, borough of Tatahulcapan, Xalapa. Tel: 228/818 55 23, fax: 817 24 59, www.hotelesenxalapa.com
***Hotel Posada Coatapec*. Colonial charm and innovative and astonishingly inexpensive restaurant. Hidalgo 9, Coatapec center. Tel: 228/816 05 44, fax: 816 00 40, www.posadacoatapec.com.mx

Must See
Great variety in local cultural life of Xalapa. The Orquestra Sinfónica enjoys international reputation. The Museo de Antropologia in Xalapa is situated on the university campus. Rafting in Jalcomulco about 45 minutes from Coatapec.

Local Attractions
San Carlos de Perote Fortress in the town of El Perote. Located at an altitude of about 2,400 meters (7,870 feet) approx. 50 km (31 miles) from Xalapa at the foot of the Cofre de Perote volcano.
Orizaba: colonial jewel and important industrial center. San Miguel Parish Church and the strangely designed town hall (originally the Belgian pavilion at the 1889 World Exhibition) are also worth seeing.
Fortín de las Flores: town situated 6 km (4 miles) to the west of Córdoba, famous for its mild climate and flowers. The zócalo, consisting of two equal-sized parks, is also wonderful. Fantastic view onto the Pico de Orizaba on clear days.

Information
Secretaría de Turismo, Blvd. Cristóbal Colón No. 5, Torre Animas, Fracc. Jardines de las Animas, Xalapa. Tel: 228/841 85 00, ext. 4330, 228/841 85 41, toll-free number for domestic calls: 01-800/712 66 66, e-mail: subtur@sedecover.gob.mx

The City of Artists – Oaxaca
The Colonial Pearl and its Aficionados

Magical, mystical, picturesque, and lively: such is Oaxaca, the colonial pearl in Mexico's south that has inspired innumerable artists. Oaxaca is famous for its traditional arts and crafts and its unique church.

Impressed by Oaxaca's remarkable colonial character, UNESCO declared the town a World Heritage Site in 1987. Situated at a height of 1,600 meters (5,350 feet), Oaxaca is famous not only for its splendidly baroque churches and monasteries but also for the large number of artists resident here – and not only for their artistic commitment and presence but also for the inspiration they bring to bear in other areas: Francisco Toledo, for example, became involved himself in social welfare projects that created jobs to help sustain traditional skilled worker's trades.

The first impetus came from the now-deceased father of Mexican modern art, Rufino Tamayo, who bequeathed a collection of pre-Hispanic objets d'art to his native town in 1974. These are on display in a colonial manor house in the Avenida Morelos 503. A museum for contemporary art followed – also located in a magnificent town mansion on Macedonio Alcalá (503). The Oaxaca State Graphic Arts Institute (Macedonio Alcalá 507), founded in 1988 by the painter Francisco Toledo, completes the triumvirate of artistic institutions all situated in close proximity to one another. The Institute's holdings include not only the graphic work of famous Mexican painters from Diego Rivera to Guadalupe Posada but also work by Salvador Dalí and Francisco Goya.

Oaxaca's most famous colonial building is the restored Santo Domingo Monastery, also situated in the Macedonio Alcalá. The church interior is a sensually overwhelming baroque spectacle with a stupendous "Dominican Family Tree" made of colored stucco. The Museo de las Culturas in the adjacent monastery boasts a special collection of valuable historical documents including finds from tomb no. 7 in the Olmec metropolis Monte Albán. Located about eight kilometers (5 miles) from Oaxaca, it is a much loved and most important local attraction.

1 Santo Domingo Church in Oaxaca, one of the most beautiful churches in Mexico.
2 Guelaguetza show in the Hotel Camino Real.
3 Denuded mountains and cacti characterize Oaxaca's surroundings.
4 The monumental Zapotec city of Monte Albán.

1 Restaurant and café on Oaxaca's zócalo.
2 Hotel Casa Cid de León.
3 and **4** Colorful and spectacular: the Guelaguetza show in the historic setting of the Hotel Camino Real in Oaxaca.

Cultural life vibrates in numerous galleries and arts and crafts enterprises. Workshops and salesrooms in the town center invite you to rummage through their stocks in search of that special piece of traditional craftsmanship: handmade paper, embroidery based on old-fashioned samplers, and vegetable dyes. Amateur painters exhibit their "Sunset over Monte Albán" next to schoolchildren's efforts on the topic of "The Colonial Bridge." There is always an opportunity to pop into one of the many cafés between all these temples of art. And don't forget to visit the "La Soledad" chocolate shop in the Calle Mina or some of the jewelry shops dotted around the town like confetti. In one such goldsmith's workshop in 5 de Mayo on the corner of Murguia, Antonio Ramos

Rojas elucidates the four different earring shapes: the lyre, or lira, the chandelier, the basket, and the little worm – gusanito. Smooth or riffled, decorated with precious stones or with pearls or corals, they are real eye-catchers.

It is no wonder that the local cuisine is also an artistic product. The Market on 20 de Noviembre street is stocked with produce supplied by the Zapotec women from the surrounding villages: moles are sauces made from chocolate, chilies, seeds, nuts, and almonds and mixed with stewed tomatoes – delicious! Pyramids of shiny jars with moles in curry yellow, dark brown, and brick red tower next to plaited bunches of local cheese, queso de Oaxaca. A typical breakfast in Oaxaca consists of a sauce made of squash blossoms and served with homemade quesadillas (tortillas filled with cheese) alongside a cup of steaming hot chocolate. If you can't get yourself invited to a homemade breakfast by one of the locals, console yourself on the tastefully designed patio of the

Camino Real restaurant in the former monastery of Santa Catalina, now a first-class hotel in Calle 5 de Mayo. Their hot chocolate and quesadillas, served in hand-painted local ceramic dishes, are (nearly) just as good. Another local specialty requires a bit of a sense of adventure: the chapulines served by Indian women are dried grasshoppers – an unusual source of protein. And the gusanito, the little worm, also plays a role in a local specialty and proves that the Mexcal liquor has the alcohol content that it claims; one such little worm lies at the bottom of each Mexcal bottle. Whoever gets it when the last dregs have been poured must drink up without hesitating – this, too, is art.

The Casa Cid de León has four suites available for those who might have overindulged in the Mexcal. Sleeping here is like being transported back 100 years – but in luxury. Antiques, lace covers, candelabras, grandfather clocks, and typically Mexican flowers recall Mexico's Belle Époque for your delectation.

Oaxaca – City of Artists

Getting there and when to travel
Air: frequent flights from Mexico City and Puerto Escondido.
Bus: first-class bus terminal: Av. Niños Héroes, second-class: Periférico West.
Best travel time: all year. Rainy season from May to September.

Where to stay
****Casa Cid de León*, Av. Morelos 602, Oaxaca 68000.
Tel: 951/514 11 02, www.casaciddeleon.com
**** *Hotel Camino Real*, 5 Av. De Mayo 300. Tel: 951/501 61 00, fax: 516 07 32, www.camino-real-oaxaca.com
***Hotel Las Golondrinas*, Tinoco y Palacios 411.
Tel: 951/514 32 98, fax: 514 21 26, centrally located with a quiet, idyllic patio.

Must See
Zócalo with wrought-iron band pavilion, Alameda, cathedral, and former monastery of Santo Domingo. Numerous churches and monasteries; San José monastery houses the art school. Markets: Mercado Benito Juárez and Arts and Crafts Market, also Mercado 20 de Noviembre. The Guelaguetza feast is celebrated in July according to Zapotec traditions. Local participation and cooperation. Effusive dance festivals, processions, theater.

Local Attractions
Colorful markets in Zaachila (Thursdays), Santo Tomás Jalieza, Ocotlán de Morelos (Fridays), Tlacolula (Sundays).

Construction of the Zapotec pyramid city Monte Albán began in the 5th century BC. Up to 30,000 inhabitants lived here during its heyday between 100 and 500 AD. Monte Albán rises above a sierra landscape on a specially constructed plateau measuring 200 by 300 meters (660 by 980 feet). Some of the Olmec palaces and pyramids are decorated with relief work that shows grotesquely gesturing people – possibly dancers or prisoners. The Olmec culture declined around 800 AD. 400 years later, the Mextecs used Monte Albán as a ceremonial center. The most beautiful view is from the platform.
Mitla: situated about 40 km (25 miles) away, a former Zapotec ceremonial center probably used as a city of the dead from 1000 AD onwards. Five sets of buildings have been excavated. The geometric ornamental friezes and the stark, windowless walls of the former palaces as well as the Grupo de las Columnas mosaics are particularly impressive.
Hieve al Agua: a wonderful sight: a stone waterfall after which the park is named. Specially laid-out walking paths and bathing opportunities complete the experience.

Information
Av. Independencia 607. Tel: 951/516 01 23,
e-mail: info@oaxaca.gob.mx and information kiosks at the airport.

Two Sides to Every Story
Acapulco – the Legend

Much money has been invested in Acapulco over the last year to recreate its former glory and help it compete with its great rival – Cancún. The venture has been successful. Smart hotels, chic discos, and top-class restaurants attract visitors to the lively metropolis on Mexico's most beautiful bay.

Cradled in hammocks, we look out over the Pacific and watch the breakers come crashing onto sand as white as icing sugar. Our hostess at the Hacienda Vayma Resort calls us in for breakfast, a traditional mix of fresh fruit and a generous portion of huevos rancheros, fried eggs with tomatoes on a fried tortilla. There's no point in counting calories when you're on holiday in Mexico … the parrots squawk away under the palm trees and we conclude our morning's meditations by the sea, shake the sand from our feet, and follow the tempting smells that beckon us inside.

The fishing village of Pie de la Cuesta, situated about 10 kilometers (6 miles) to the northwest of the paradisiacal bay of Acapulco on the Coyuca Lagoon promontory, comes pretty close to providing the ideal beach holiday: quiet, secluded, tranquil. The fish are cleaned every morning so thoroughly that their scales glitter, siestas are held every afternoon, and should the inclination take you, thirst can be quenched with the milk of a freshly picked coconut as you while away the hours in your hammock. The splendid sunsets over kilometers of dead straight beach that stretch into the distance are the main event of the day.

Nonetheless, with all due respect for the pacific peace that Pie de la Cuesta offers, everybody wants to see Acapulco. The name automatically evokes jet set, divorce dramas, diamond gifts, unfaithful lovers, playboys, Liz Taylor, Lana Turner, Lex Barker, Errol Flynn, Cary Grant, John Wayne, and, above all, Johnny Weissmüller. Who could forgo all this – even if the tiger-skin barstools in Teddy Stauffer's La Perla Bar have long since become the stuff of moth-eaten legend?

So, it's off to Acapulco. The reality of today's city comprises a population of two million and three distinct characters: the slightly decayed old town situated around the zócalo with its girdle of

1 View from Condessa Beach, Acapulco Bay, onto Las Brisas.
2 Cheerful musicians.
3 Head of the feathered serpent by Diego Rivera.
4 View from the Bellavista Restaurant near Las Brisas onto old Acapulco and the island of La Roqueta.

1 Legendary: the cliff divers of Acapulco.
2 Remote and untouched: beach near Petatlán on the Pacific coast of Guerrero.
3 View from Las Brisas onto the island of La Roqueta in Acapulco Bay.
4 La Quebrada cliffs: villas built by American film stars still stand here.
5 A busy day on the beach of Acapulco.

mango trees and its very own feeling of milieu; the older Playa Caleta; and last but not least, the tourist metropolis with everything the heart desires: fast-food kiosks, Wal-Mart stores, branches of the GAP clothing store, cocktail bars, hotels in every size and shape, discos, sandy beaches, and souvenir shops on Avenida Miguel Alemán. We've seen enough and turn our backs on the synthetic holiday atmosphere.

Stepping into the foyer of the Hotel Los Flamingos we enter a famous relic from a golden age. In the early 1950s, Acapulco served as a hideaway from tinsel town for Johnny Weissmüller and the Hollywood Gang that hung around with him. Johnny discovered it whilst filming some scenes for one of his Tarzan films in nearby Laguna de Tres Palos. He fell in love – forever and so deeply that the Hotel Los Flamingos, small and modest and painted in a rich hue of Mexican pink, soon changed hands. Along with his

buddies John Wayne and Red Skelton, the five-time Olympic gold medal winner and most famous Tarzan of all times bought Los Flamingos. It is situated high up in a natural amphitheater of jungle and rocks that encircles the idyllic natural harbor.

A long time ago, this natural harbor would have combined the scents of both the Near and the Far East: it would have glistened like Asian silk, shone like Chinese porcelain, and sparkled like jewels from all four corners of the world. Then again, it would have stunk like the sewers of Paris and trembled under the blows of hammers wielded by carpenters and Spanish shipbuilders who built their first caravels here as early as 1532. In the Aztec Náhuatl language, Acapulco means "the place of waving reeds." It was here that the treasures imported from Asian ports and from Spain's eastern colonies were unloaded onto the backs of donkeys that transported the exotic delicacies 900 kilometers (560 miles) across country to Veracruz on the Gulf of Mexico, there to be reloaded onto ships and taken across the ocean to Spain. There is more history in Acapulco than in any other Mexican harbor. And now it has more hotels than any other: happily, the plans for new hotel zones on the Bahía de Puerto Marqués seem unlikely to repeat earlier building sins in the bay itself.

Johnny Weissmüller and his mates must take some responsibility for the sudden popularity of the Mexican Pacific coast. Whilst Tarzan-Johnny was probably relaxing in his hammock by the Casa Redonda on the premises of the Hotel Los Flamingos, maybe slurping a coco loco (coconut milk, lemonade, rum, and tequila that was first mixed together right here) from a coconut, the building cranes were being wheeled into place, and the first spades flashed as work began on hotels that were soon to compete with Los Flamingos. But not one of them can hold a candle to Los Flamingos. None of them has yellowing paparazzi photos in the hotel lobby showing Hollywood stars. And none of them has the Casa Redonda, in which Johnny lived until his death in 1984. Even if the rooms have showers and no bathtubs: Los Flamingos and its bartenders, Juan and Santiago, are legends.

Then the rich came to Acapulco: the rocky landscape is home to estates owned by Sylvester Stallone, Elizabeth Taylor, and Julio Iglesias. Attracted by all this wealth, the not-so-rich also made their way here to take a look at the rich and famous and the way they lived. Mirrors in the lobby, hidden luxury, women hiding behind huge sunglasses: it's all still here. But mass tourism has swept over the bay of Acapulco and now sets the tone.

1 Good, hearty food at the El Zorrito Restaurant in Acapulco.
2 Round bungalow in the Los Flamingos Hotel in Acapulco.
3 The Beach Club of Hotel Las Brisas in Acapulco.
4 Work with a view: waiter in the Bella Vista Restaurant near Las Brisas.
5 Natural: eating and drinking in the 100% Natural Restaurant in Acapulco.

There is just one place left where the rumble and roar of modern tourism remains unwelcome: the cliffs from which the cliff divers plunge into a little bay that is not much bigger than a bathtub. First introduced 60 years ago, this spectacle is highly dangerous. To start with, the cliffs are 37 meters (120 feet) high. They do not rise at a right angle but jut out further at the base. Divers must take this factor into consideration as well as calculating the ebb and flow of the waves that the sea sends into the rocky bay. Many clavadistas have to overcome their fear as they approach the diving spot, having prayed beforehand for divine protection at little altars set up on the beach. Booing, clapping, inattention on the part of the spectators – each one of whom has paid about 15 dollars to watch – disturbs the divers' concentration and is most unwelcome. The cliff divers founded their own club. Every diver who has

performed one good dive generally considered worth watching is eligible for membership. It is said that at the beginning, they egged each other on to dive from spots higher up the cliff. It turned into a kind of macho competition in which courage was equated with manliness, until the first diver plunged from the highest cliff spot in 1934. The Swiss bandleader, Teddy Stauffer, had the La Perla nightclub built opposite the diving rocks in the early 1960s. The entrance fee comprised two drinks – and a view of the diving show taking place across the bay. Johnny Weissmüller, the best swimmer of his time, was tempted to try the dive – a wish that probably brought his Hollywood producers perilously close to a heart attack and was therefore never realized. Before we return to Pie de la Cuesta for our own coco loco at sunset, we persuade a taxi driver to take us into the mountains to look at the monumental fresco that Diego Rivera put together in the 1950s with shells, tile fragments, and stones. It covers the outside wall of a villa that once belonged to Dolores Olmedo, one of his numerous muses, and shows the feathered serpent Quetzalcóatl and Tepezcuincle, the dog of the gods. The archaic and the modern still lie close by one another in today's Mexico.

Acapulco – two sides to the pleasure story

Getting there and when to travel
Air: international and charter flights to Acapulco airport, 22 km (14 miles) east of the city. Frequent flights from Mexico City and Oaxaca.
Bus: approx. five-hour bus trip on the Autopista del Sol from Mexico City to Acapulco. Numerous connections along the Pacific coast as far as Puerto Escondido.
Best travel time: October to May. It can get very hot and humid during the rainy season in summer.

Where to stay
*****Hotel Elcano*, Av. Costera Miguel Alemán 75. Tel: 744/435 15 00, fax: 484 22 30, www.hotel-elcano.com, spacious, comfortable hotel on the beach, once a favorite of

the stars, completely redesigned and modernized.
***Los Flamingos*, Av. López Mateos, Fracc. Las Playas. Tel: 744/482 06 90, fax: 483 98 06, www.acapulco-hotels-online.com, former home to the stars of the 1950s, 46 rooms, not all with air-conditioning.
***El Mirador*, Plazoleta La Quebrada 74. Tel: 744/483 11 55, fax: 482 45 04, built into the cliffs with three picturesque little pools. View from the restaurant terraces directly onto the clavadistas diving from the cliffs.

Must See
The high cliff divers of La Quebrada show their skills for the paying public, every diver jumping three to five times a day at set times: at noon, and four times in the evening and at night. The Parque Acuático located on Costero Miguel Alemán is great for children: dolphin shows and adventure swimming pools. The Mundo Mágico Marino is another adventure theme park with aquarium and museum. The Aqua Zoo is situated on the Isla La Roqueta: ferry service with glass-bottom boats. Beaches: La Condesa for seeing and being seen, has become more popular than the more traditional beaches of La Caleta and La Caletilla. The sea is calmer in Puerto Marqués. Nightlife addresses: Andromeda, Babe's on the Costera, and Enigma and Palladium on Carretera Escénica above the coastline.

Local Attractions
10 kilometers (6 miles) to the bay of Pipe de la Cuesta, famous for its high waves. Other coves accessible via Mex 200. Day trip to Taxco.

Information
www.guerrero.gob.mx, www.acapulco-travel.web.com. Oficina de Convenciones y Visitantes de Acapulco, Costera Miguel Alemán 38. Tel: 744/484 85 55

From Fishing Village to Holiday Fun
Puerta Vallarta – Destiny Came by Way of a Film

Once upon a time, there were only fishers here: then John Huston came along and filmed "The Night of the Iguana" in Puerta Vallarta. Since then, the town has grown into one of Mexico's most important bathing resorts without losing any of its Mexican charms. Its Hinterland is a paradise for eco- and adventure tourists.

There was a time when Mexican landscapes were especially popular with Hollywood directors. While Johnny Weissmüller was filming Tarzan in the Laguna de Tres Palos near Acapulco, John Huston chose Puerta Vallarta to film "The Night of the Iguana". That was 1963: the star of the film was Richard Burton, and Elizabeth Taylor accompanied him. They had just fallen in love and their affair made the town more famous than the film itself.

And so the fishing village of Puerta Vallarta was roused from its slumbers. Until 1956, there had not even been a telephone connection or electricity in the wide sweep of the Bahía de Banderas (Bay of Flags) – never mind a road connection to Guadalajara, the capital of the state of Jalisco. Today, it takes five hours to get through the mountains down to the sea: an enchanting journey that takes visitors through a tropical mist jungle. The flight takes only 35 minutes.

Naturally, the Bahía de Banderas looks completely different today to the way it did in the 1960s, with an impressive array of hotels down by the beach, approximately 1 million seaside guests per annum, and about 30,000 beds. Puerto Vallarta is Mexico's second-biggest Pacific resort and consists of two parts: the modern hotel suburbs of Nuevo Vallarta and Marina Vallarta in the northern part of Banderas Bay that is actually located in the state of Nayarit, and the older, much expanded Puerto Vallarta in Jalisco. But this division does not disturb the harmony of the old harbor town on the Río Cuale with its cobbled alleys and colonial brick church of Nuestra Señora de Guadalupe. Its special local charm remains one of its main attractions.

Today, the entire region is referred to as the Costa Vallarta. It is characterized by a breathtaking variety of landscape: coming from the north, the coastline consists of 40 kilometers (25 miles) of

1 Golf course, Hotel Four Seasons Resorts in Punta Mita.
2 View onto Mismaloya where John Huston filmed "The Night of the Iguana" in 1962/63 with Ava Gardner and Richard Burton.
3 Swimming with dolphins.
4 Mismaloya Bay.

1 Charming: Puerto Vallarta.
2 "Ana Gabriela" room in Hotel Villa del Sol in Zihuatanejo.
3 Beach at the Hotel Four Seasons Resorts in Punta Mita.
4 Hotel Quinta María Cortéz Bed and Breakfast.

curving bays, steep cliffs, peaceful sandy beaches under palm trees, and riverbeds whose colorful stone beds sparkle in the sun. In between lie islands of tropical forests, out of which orange helicons and bird of paradise flowers shine. Now and then, a little bit of Mexican desert makes an appearance.

The local hotels are just as diverse. Those not interested in beachside accommodation might choose to stay in the Hacienda San Angel. The view from the terrace is spectacular – the little iron crown on the top of Nuestra Señora Cathedral in Guadalupe appears almost close enough to touch. The somewhat unusual shape of the crown is said to derive from the shape of Empress Charlotte's crown. The Hacienda San Angel is situated in the middle of the old town, door-to-door with smart eateries and art galleries. It comprises three separate villas with massive balconies and tiled roofs that have been restored in the colonial style. Richard Burton bought one of these villas – not for Liz, but for a woman with whom he later had a more peaceful marriage: Susan

Burton. We walk through the grounds between tropical flower beds on paths that connect the three villas and nine suites with one another. The furnishings testify to an old-school approach to quality: marble floors, wonderful old family portraits, antiques, and carefully selected Mexican arts and crafts. The hacienda is situated near the popular Playa Las Mulas and has three swimming pools.

There could hardly be a greater contrast to Majahuitas – a boutique hotel à la Robinson situated between palm trees directly on the beach, about 20 minutes by boat away from Puerto Vallarta itself. The Mexican palapas served as design model for the Majahuitas establishment – palm-leaf-covered open houses with whitewashed walls. This Mayan architecture is typical for the terra caliente, the hot zone, and can often be seen on the Yucatán peninsular and in Chetumal. Terraces and platforms are used to structure the overall design and provide additional space. Those who choose Majahuitas are looking for peace and relaxation without superfluous comfort. There are no lights – just candles and lanterns. Swimming and diving in underwater canyons as well as an excursion to the tropical jungle are part of the package.

Domesticated nature and relaxing tranquility: such is the concept of the exclusive hotel Four Seasons Punta Mita on the northern edge of the Bahía de Banderas. The large pool seems directly connected to the sea; plants are used to add some decorative color. The walls are so white that they seem to be in competition with the snow-white sand in front of the hotel entrance. Don't miss the resort's unique attraction: a golf course designed by Jack Nicklaus on a little peninsular.

Puerto Vallarta – destiny came by way of a film

Getting there and when to travel
Air: the international airport is situated about 7 km (4 miles) from Puerto Vallarta and provides good national connections with Aeroméxico and Mexicana. North American airlines also fly to the airport.
Bus: the new and busy Super Central Cemionera bus terminal is situated to the north of the airport.
Best travel time: November to May. Rainy season between June and October.

Where to stay
*****Four Seasons Punta Mita*, Punta Mita, Bahía de Banderas. Tel: 329/291 60 00, fax: 291 60 60, www.fourseasons.com, 42 km (26 miles) to the north of Puerto Vallarta with its own golf course on a small peninsular, jumbo suites, cultural center, kids program, spa, luxurious.
****Hacienda San Angel*, Miramar 336, e-mail: sanangel@mexicoboutiquehotels.com, nine rooms in three villas, three separate swimming pools, terraces.
***Majahuitas*, 13 km (8 miles) south of Puerto Vallarta. Contact via majahuitas@mexicoboutiquehotels.com, eight houses accessible only by boat, traditional building style.

Must See
Remains of the former film set for The Night of the Ignuana in Mismaloya; very good restaurants nearby. The mountain town of San Francisco del Oeste in the Sierra Madre. The Costa Careyes, an insider tip, to the south of Puerto Vallartes on the so-called Costa Alegre ("happy coast") has a unique situation on a hilly coastline.

Local Attractions
To the north and the south of Puerto Valarta: interesting fishing villages of Las Animas, Quimixto and Xelapa accessible only with taxi boats. Xelapa has become a favorite place amongst the artistic bohemians. More beaches at Las Conchas and Las Chinas. Two days should be set aside for a visit to Guadalajara.

Information
Palacio Municipal, Juárez. Tel: 332/224 11 75, www.visit-puertovallarta.gob.mx, www.nayarit.gob.mx

Riding the Waves
Ixtapa and Zihuatanejo

Mountains covered in dense tropical vegetation and dramatic cliffs are the scenic backdrop to Zihuatanejo and its smart holiday paradise, Ixtapa, where mile upon mile of sandy beaches lined with palm trees stretch into the distance — and waves that every surfer dreams of crash onto the coast.

The pre-Spanish Tarasc kings knew where to come and relax: in Zihuatanejo — which means "dark woman" in Náhuatl, the language originally spoken by the indigenous population. It is said that King Tagáxoan II Caltzontzín came here to this horseshoe-shaped bay on the Pacific for the winter months. For a short period during the colonial era, the Spaniards used the bay as a trade harbor. Finally, in the 1960s, tourists discovered the sleepy fishing village and its perfect beaches.

The former fishing village is situated in the paradisiacal Bahía de Zihuatanejo and is now a small town with nearly 40,000 inhabitants and an important port of call for cruise liners. Ixtapa is situated about ten kilometers (6 miles) to the northwest of Zihuatanejo. Like Cancún, it started out on the drawing board about 30 years ago: a settlement comprising luxury hotels, a golf club, an exclusive yacht harbor, and a lagoon in which small crocodiles sun themselves, rearing up suddenly to lunge at a passing bird.

Despite the commercial development that goes hand in hand with tourism, Zihautanejo has managed to retain much of its old charm. Walking around the harbor or in the streets, you'll see Mexican families holidaying here with kids and grandparents, as well as fishers and tradesmen. In the Mercado de las Artesanías, the vendors are so keen to sell their wares — silver from Taxco and colorfully painted ceramics or tree-bark paintings — that they constantly lower their prices in the hope of making a sale. The bars and cafés in the pedestrian zone are ideal for indulging in some people-watching as holidaymakers the color of lobsters stroll past. Between them are backpackers from all over the world, happy to have found a cheaper alternative to the luxury hotels in a local bed-and-breakfast hostel.

1 Like a pyramid sitting on a hill: the Westin Brisas in Ixtapa.
2 Sun, sand, and coconut palms: the beach at the Villa del Sol in Zihuatanejo.
3 Synonymous with luxury: hammock by the pool in the Villa del Sol.
4 Zihuatanejo Bay.

The Villa del Sol is not just a luxury hotel, it's a dream! The native German Helmut Leins fulfilled his dream when he opened up the boutique hotel on La Ropa beach in Zihuatanejo: a dream that his guests can now dream for themselves. 70 rooms and suites, tastefully furnished with Mexican furniture and art, are situated in a splendid garden with several pools. Lying in a hammock, we are lulled to sleep by the sound of the waves and the wind in the palms. Why leave – ever? Small wonder that the hotel belongs to the group of "Small Luxury Hotels of the World" and has won several prizes, including a place on the prestigious Condé Nast Traveler's list of "Best Places to Stay in the Whole World."

But leave we must: Zihuatanejo and its surroundings are waiting to be discovered. We follow the advice provided by Helmut Leins' friendly hotel staff and take the winding road northwards towards the Playa de los Troncones – an El Dorado for surfers. The massive waves are not a sight for the fainthearted: clearly not a problem for surfers. We prefer to watch them from a safe distance, seated in the comfort of a beach restaurant with a glass of sparkling limonada de limón and a ceviche seafood cocktail. Life is good.

In the afternoon, we drive on to Ixtapa. A panorama of modern hotels sitting side by side with splendid pool landscapes stretches away into the distance. A walk along the beach soon explains why more people are swimming in the pools than the ocean: the waves

1 Beach idyll at the Villa del Sol in Zihuatenejo.
2 Restaurant and bar La Catina in the Villa del Sol.
3 Suite in the Villa del Sol.
4 Mexico pure: Casa Elvira restaurant in Zihuatanejo.
5 Exotic drinks in La Cantina – it's not far to bed afterwards.

are high but the currents are even more dangerous. You have to be a good, strong swimmer not to be dragged down by the undertow. Every swimmer should check the flag status on the beach. "Black" means danger. The fact that Ixtapa was built by the

National Development Association FONATUR is obvious from the clean, well-kept streets and alleys. We just make it to the Villa de la Selva before sundown. Once the home of a Mexican president, it is now a romantic restaurant with a breathtaking view over the wide Bay of Ixtapa. From here, we watch a picture-book sunset. Later on, we return to the hustle and bustle of Zihuatanejo. The restaurant and bar La Sirena Gorda serves not only the best fish tacos in town; it is also the best place to get the latest information on surfing, diving, and fishing.

Ixtapa and Zihuatanejo – riding the waves

Getting there and when to travel

Air: from Mexico City with Aeroméxico and Mexicana. Several North American airlines also fly to the local airport.
Car and Bus: regular bus service from Mexico City (Central de Autobuses del Sur Taxqueña) with Estrella de Oro and Futura services to Zihuatanejo via Acapulco. Estrella Blanca and Estrella de Oro provide services from Acapulco itself. Beautiful but winding coastal road to Zihuatanejo. Numerous topes (speed-bumps) mean slow progress. The 240-km (149 miles) journey can take up to five hours.
Best travel time: November to May. Rainy season between June and October/November. Short spells of heavy rain in the afternoon.

Where to stay

*****Hotel Villa del Sol*, Playa de la Ropa, 40880 Ixtapa-Zihuatanejo. Tel: 755/555 55 00, fax: 554 27 58, e-mail: hotel@villa-sol.com.mx, www.villasol.com.mx
****Hotel The Westin Brisas Resort Ixtapa (formerly Camino Real)*. Exclusive holiday resort with 428 rooms spread over 12 floors arranged like a pyramid. Playa Vista Hermosa, 40888 Ixtapa-Zihuatanejo. Tel: 755/32 232, fax: 30 751, e-mail: ublado.fierros@westin.com, www.westin.com

***Hotel El Tradicional (formerly Villa Hera)*. Situated in the center of Zihuatanejo, 45 comfortable rooms, Av. Morelos No. 165, 40880 Zihuatanejo. Tel: 755/554 29 20, fax: 554 85 15, e-mail: villaverazih@prodigy.net.mx, www.ixtapa-zihuatanejo.net/eltradicioinal

Must See

International guitar festival, always in April. Cockfights in the surrounding villages, above all in Los Troncones.

Local Attractions

Boat trips to the offshore islands of Isla Ixtapa, Isla de la Pie, and Isla Grande as well as to the bird sanctuary Morro de los Pericos. For snorkeling: Las Cuatas beach. Remains of a stone wall originally built by a Tarasc King in pre-Spanish times can be viewed here.

Information

Oficina de Convenciones y Visitantes de Ixtapa-Zihuatanejo (OCVIZ), Paseo de las Gaviotas 12, Ixtapa.
Tel : 755/553 12 70, e-mail: info@ixtapa-zihuatanejo.org
Oficina de Turismo, Zihuatanejo town hall (center).
Tel : 755/554 20 01, e-mail: 755/554 20 01,
e-mail: turismozihixt@prodigy.net.mx

Paradise for Eco-tourists
The Waterfalls at Agua Azul and Misol-Ha

There is an unbelievable variety of flora and fauna in Chiapas. Seven different eco-systems exist here side by side – including those at Agua Azul and Misol-Ha, the colossal Sumidero Canyon and the lagoons of Montebello.

W hy should I go to the zoo in Mexico?" my girlfriend asks me dumbfounded when we arrive in Tuxtla Gutiérrez, the capital of Mexico's southernmost state, Chiapas. She couldn't believe that I'd insisted on coming all the way here just for a zoo that seemed to offer few attractions for tourists – at first glance. But the Miguel Álvarez del Toro zoological garden in Zapotal Park is considered one of the best of its kind. Amidst an abundant and verdant plant life, it houses only animals that are native to this part of the world, including jaguars and tapirs, many species of bird, such as the tucal and the quetzal, serpents such as the boa and the rattlesnake, and reptiles such as caimans and crocodiles. At midday, when the sun is hottest, I drag her to the shady oasis provided by the Dr Faustino Miranda Botanical Gardens for the next set of surprises. In addition to comprehensive information on the region's diverse vegetation, the garden also boasts a significant collection of medicinal plants. Originally used by none other than the Maya, their healing properties guarantee their continued popularity today. There is even a center for Mayan medicine in San Cristóbal de las Casas where shamans cure all manner of ailments. And there is no excuse for boredom in the evening either: my girlfriend is fascinated by the elderly couples who still swing their hips skillfully to the marimba rhythms in the pretty little Marimba Park – some compensation for the strenuous day of immersion in the natural sciences.

"Wow!" she says, next morning, as we stop on the Belisario Domínguez Bridge on the way to Chiapa de Corzo. Stretching across the Grijalva River at a vertiginous height, it marks the beginning of the colossal Sumidero Canyon. With a maximum depth of 1,000 meters (3,300 feet), the canyon is one of the most impressive geological fissures in South America. It starts

1 Only local animals are kept in the zoo at Tuxtla Gutiérrez.
2 Waterfalls at Misol-Ha: 30 meters (100 feet) of free fall.
3 Sunbathing: an iguana in the zoo at Tuxtla Gutiérrez.
4 Almost like David and Goliath: tourists contemplate the immense Sumidero Canyon.

1 Fun in the water near the Agua Azul waterfalls.
2 Breeding turtles in the zoo at Tuxtla Gutiérrez.
3 It's easy to get down to the pool at the bottom of the Misol-Ha waterfalls.
4 The river cascades into rocky pools in Agua Azul.
5 A Christmas tree made of stone: the "Arbol de Navidad" in the Sumidero Canyon.

23 kilometers (14 miles) to the south of Tuxtla Gutiérrez and ends 42 kilometers (26 miles) later in the Chicoasén reservoir, where a power station uses the water pressure to supply most of southern Mexico with electricity. Coming from Tuxtla Gutiérrez, it is possible to view the canyon from the comfort of an asphalted road. Along the way lie the panorama vantage points of La Ceiba, La Coyuta, El Tepehuaje, and El Roblar – all of which also have a camping site – and Los Chiapa, where you can sample the diverse regional cuisine. But it is more exciting by far to take a speedboat through the gorge. It leaves from the idyllic little town of Chiapa de Corzo, situated 14 kilometers (9 miles) to the south of Tuxtla Gutiérrez on the banks of the Río Grijalva. At Villahermosa in the state of

5

Tabasco, this river joins up with the Río Usumacinta and flows into the Gulf of Mexico. For the time being, we take our place in the modern speedboats moored at the jetties that quickly fill up with tourists putting on the obligatory safety jackets. Water sprays up around us as we pick up speed and then stop suddenly to look at caves, waterfalls, and impressive geological formations such as the so-called "Christmas tree" (Arbol de Navidad), which really does look like a mummified, decorated, stone pine tree. According to legend, the entire Chiapas tribe, including women and children, plunged to their deaths from the canyon's highest point rather than submit to enslavement by the approaching Spanish conquistadors. Continuing onwards through the canyon, we watch the big, fat vultures sitting on bare branches down by the river and smaller crocodiles that stretch their snouts out of the shallow water by the banks, waiting for some small, unsuspecting bird to pass by before snapping it up before our eyes.

In the spring of 2003, the Sumidero Eco- and Adventure National Park was opened here, and since then it has been possible to rent kayaks and mountain bikes. The same Xcaret group that manages the eco-adventure parks along Mexico's Caribbean coast in Xcaret, Tulum, and El Garrafón operates this park as well. Critics accuse the group of turning Mexico into a kind of natural Disneyland but that is far from the truth. On the contrary, the parks provide visitors with exciting opportunities to explore regional culture and nature in combination with sporting activities. The local inhabitants are employed as park guards, guides, sales persons, or service providers. The speedboats, for example, belong to a cooperative. Here, in Mexico's poorest state, tourism has become a major source of income. The eco-parks also fulfill an important educational purpose, creating a greater awareness of the importance of sustaining local culture and the environment.

A magnificent color spectacle awaits visitors in the south of Chiapas – an area bordering onto Guatemala: the Lagunas de Montebello National Park. One small lake adjoins the next and each has its own special color. The lagoons developed from

cenotes (sinkholes) whose walls simply dissolved over time. The variation in colors results from the different-colored lake bottoms – as well as from the vegetation and the light conditions, which change several times a day. The lagoons of La Esmeralda, La Encantade, Bosque Azul, Ensueño, and Antiguo are accessible via asphalt roads. Dense pine forests surround others. An unfinished road takes one to the lakes of Montebello, Cañada, Pojoj, Tziscao, and Dos Lagunas. El Tziscao lake is situated directly on the border with Guatemala.

The route from San Cristóbal de las Casas to Palenque is one of the most beautiful in the country. It starts in the cool highlands and winds its way through coffee plantations in the tropical forests. The stupendously impressive Agua Azul waterfalls are situated 64 kilometers (40 miles) before Palenque, the city whose name stems from the legendary Mayan site.

The Agua Azul River flows into the Bascán River here in a series of tremendous cascades. Some of the natural pools are accessible for bathers. Those that present a real danger to life and limb are clearly marked with large signs. Quite a few tourists have drowned here in the rushing whirlpools. There are many restaurants set in the dense vegetation that lines the paths by the waterfalls, all offering delicious fish dishes. It's a great opportunity to relax and watch the local Mayan children helping their traditionally costumed mothers to sell sweets and arts and crafts products.

Agua Azul also has good camping opportunities. No traces remain of the Zapatista rebels who led an insurgence against the government from their base in the jungle around Agua Azul on January 1, 1994 – but there are plenty of military patrols. Traveling around Agua Azul is definitely not a security risk.

The next waterfall is situated 34 kilometers (21 miles) to the north of Agua Azul. Although Misol-Ha is as dramatic as Agua Azul, it is much more secluded. The water falls 30 meters (98 feet) into a natural pool that measures roughly 300 by 100 meters (980 by 330 feet) with a depth of between 80 and 200 centimeters (31 and 80 inches) – completely safe for swimmers. A cooperative recently built a small hotel here in the middle of the jungle. It has several small, comfortable huts all equipped with showers and kitchens as well as its own restaurant. The peace and quiet here is heavenly. The distant roar of the water and the birds singing in the clear, wood-scented air are music to our ears.

Agua Azul and Misol-Ha – a holidaymaker's paradise

Getting there and when to travel
Air: several flights a day from Mexico City to Tuxtla Gutiérrez as well as from Cancún via Mérida. Villahermosa, and Oaxaca. From Mexico City with Aeroméxico and Mexicana. Several North American airlines also fly to the local airport.
Bus: regular service from Mexico City direct to Tuxtla Gutiérrez. From Tuxtla Gutiérrez to San Cristóbal de las Casas and from there to Palenque.
Car: it is best to discover the region in a rental car or on a guided round-trip: Villahermosa via Palenque, Misol-Ha, Agua Azul, San Cristóbal to Tuxtla Gutiérrez or the other way around. The lagoons of Montebello can be reached via the Panamericana highway going towards Tapachula.
Best travel time: November to May.

Where to stay
***Hotel Bonampak Tuxtla*. Good, middle-class hotel, Blvd. Belisario Domínguez 180, Tuxtla Gutiérrez. Tel: 961/602 59 16, fax: 602 59 25, e-mail: hotbonam@prodigy.net.mx
***Holiday Inn*, Blvd. Belisario Domínguez 1081, Tuxtla Gutiérrez. Tel: 961/617 10 04, e-mail: dos.tgmx@wm.holiday-inn.com, www.holiday-inn.com/tuxtla

Must See
Remains of a pyramid site with Mayan and Olmec influences on the outskirts of Chiapa de Corzo. A tomb was found inside the restored, one-storey pyramid: its contents – historically important ceramics – are on show here. One of the oldest pre-Columbian sites in Mesoamerica.
The La Pila fountain in Chiapa de Corzo is one of the world's most beautiful Moorish-style colonial fountains.

Local Attractions
The El Chorreadero waterfall near Chiapa, where an underground river (in which it is possible to swim) comes gushing out of a grotto. The La Angostura reservoir is popular with anglers.
The El Aguicero waterfall in the La Venta River is situated 47 km (29 miles) to the east of Tuxtla Gutiérrez. Also ideal for observing flora and local bird species – and generally for relaxing.

Information
Blvd. Belisario Domínguez 950, Tuxtla Gutiérrez, toll-free domestic calls 01-80 02 80/35 00, e-mail: turismo@chiapas.gob.mx, www.chiapas.turista.com.mx

1 Racoon in the zoo at Tuxtla Gutiérrez.
2 Replica by Mexican artist Rina Lazo of a fresco in a temple on the Mayan site of Bonampak in the Anthropological Museum in Mexico City.
3 Immense: the waterfalls at Agua Azul.
4 Hotel Bonampak Tuxtla.

1

2

3

4

Of Mayas, Pumas, and Pirates in the Jungle
Campeche, Calakmul, Kohunlich, and Bacalar

Places of unique natural beauty and mysterious Mayan sites lie side by side in the lush tropical forest of the Chetumal region, like pearls on a string. Campeche is one of the most enchanting colonial towns in the country and rich in history.

It's a breathtaking view from the San Miguel fortress over the Gulf of Mexico – onto a sea of shining, emerald green. The impressive fort sits on a hill outside the capital city of the eponymous state on the Gulf. The robust cannons look out over the sea and no wonder – that's where the pirates came from in the 16th and 17th centuries when they arrived here to rob and pillage the most important trading port of the era: no less than Francis Drake, Henry Morgan, and Diego el Mulato (Diego the Mulatto) all put in appearances here. So, at the end of the 17th century, the city began to build a 2.5-kilometer-long (1.5 miles long) ring of fortifications with six-sided bastions and walls that were 2.5 meters (8 feet) thick and up to 8.5 meters (28 feet) tall. It was not completed until 1777 – and after that, no pirate ever dared attack Campeche again. Every week, the actors in the sight-and-sound spectacle reenact the town's history with fervor. A nightwatchman in historical costume takes us round the fortifications and their bastions, telling stories and legends of ill-starred lovers, glorious town fathers, and bloodthirsty pirates.

The town was founded in 1540 by Francisco de Mentejo the younger ("El Mozo") and given a city charter in 1777 by King Charles III of Spain. Today, the historical center is a UNESCO World Heritage Site – as are the districts of San Román, Guadalupe, and San Francisco just beyond the city center. Their narrow, cobbled alleys are lined with well-kept houses painted yellow, pale blue or green, or pink and blue, with richly ornamented balconies and spacious courtyards. No advertising signs disturb the harmonious architecture. Each of the fortresses is also worth visiting but especially San Miguel and especially in late afternoon. The museum located inside is surprisingly well stocked with spectacular local finds. The San José del Alto fortress on Bellavista

1 Idyll on Bacalar lagoon.
2 Exotic fruits, as served in the Hacienda Santa Rosa in Yucatán.
3 The jungle returns: the Mayan sites in Kohunlich near Chetumal.
4 Mysterious: the frescoes on the Chicanná pyramids in Campeche.

1 Mask of the sun god Kinich Ahau in Kohunlich.
2 The eternal rival of Tikal: Calakmul on the border with Guatemala.
3 Wild coconut palms in Kohunlich.
4 55,000 people once lived here in Calakmul, but now trees have see-
ded themselves in the ruins of the formerly majestic city.
5 Like a monster's throat: the entrance to Structure II in Chicanná.

Hill is just as impressive – a real treasure trove for fans of armor
and pirating. Besides weapons, the museum also features
reconstructed pirate ships. The San Juan bastion is devoted to
Diego the Mulatto and his fellow evildoers. La Casa 6 next to the
Parque Principal, opposite the cathedral, is a colonial and historical
treasure that houses a cultural center. The restored home that
dates from the 18th century gives visitors a glimpse into the lives
of prosperous burghers at that time.

Curious to find out what it must have been like to be the rich local
landowner, we make our way to the Hacienda Uayamón. The
former sisal hacienda, now restored, is situated about 25 kilometers to the south of Campeche, not far from the monumental
pyramid city of Edzná out in the countryside. It dates from the

17th century and is considered one of the best first-class hotels on the Yucatán peninsular. It is a dream – romantic, comfortable, refined. The former Hacienda Blanca Flor is somewhat less elegant but perhaps more authentic. It lies between Calkiní and Hecelchakán to the northeast of Campeche on the so-called King's Highway (Camino Real). Empress Charlotte, the wife of the Mexican Emperor, spent the night here about 150 years ago as she traveled to Mérida. The hacienda dates back to the 16th century. Today, it is a hotel with 20 rooms that gives us a good idea of what country life must have been like in those days. It is still run as a farming enterprise: in fact, the hacienda is more or less self-sufficient. Its owner, Dr Roberto Casillas Hernández, once held the position of private secretary to the former President José López Portillo in the early 1980s. He is also the author of important legal textbooks and works of non-fiction, including his account of the odyssey undertaken by the Shah of Iran, Reza Pahlavi, into Mexican exile. If you're lucky, you'll get the chance to sit and talk to him and his charming wife, Gilda Castellanos, over a meal or in front of the fireplace in the evening: an intellectually stimulating experience.

The important Mayan sites of Balamkú, Becán, Calakmul, Chicanná, Xpuhil, Kohunlich, and Río Bec lie between Campeche and Chetumal like pearls on a string. Start your trip around midday at the latest. The road to Chicanná via Francisco Escárcega just goes on and on. The Hotel Ecovillage Chicanná is situated directly opposite the Mayan ruins and is the starting point for all tours to Calakmul. This legendary city lies in the very heart of the Calakmul biosphere, Mexico's biggest area of tropical rainforest on the border with Guatemala. As recently as 20 years ago, it was impossible to reach Calakmul by car. Today, a narrow country round turns off the Highway 186 to Chetumal about 100 kilometers behind Escárega and from there, it's about 60 kilometers through the jungle to the city of ruins.

Between 500 and 800 AD, Calakmul was the capital of an empire that comprised several lesser Mayan cities. In its heyday between 500 and 800 AD, some 55,000 inhabitants populated Calakmul, constantly involved in warring feuds with the neighboring Tikal (in today's Guatemala) over which city was the "capital of capitals." Calakmul's end came around 850. Long periods of drought,

overpopulation, and power struggles within the Mayan empire led to a breakdown in social and political structures that also affected Calakmul itself. It fell into oblivion until the American biologist Cyrus Lundell discovered city remnants in 1931. Initially, only a few explorers came to the completely destroyed city and the jungle grew back over what had been a center of civilization. It was only in the 1990s that Mexican archeologists began excavation work again.

The core of the city was built upon a natural elevation of about 25 square kilometers (9.65 square miles) and consisted of two huge pyramids and the palace complexes that comprised courtyards and forums surrounded by buildings. The highest pyramid was reconstructed several times and now measures 45 meters (148 feet) at its highest point, which cannot be seen from the base. Those who make the effort to get to the top will be rewarded with a stupendous panoramic view over the jungle. In the late 1990s, archeologists came across a sensational find: the body of a young man aged approximately 30 years lying on a

woven grass mat in a tomb in the pyramid's interior. Ceramic vessels surrounded him; his face, chest. and hips were covered with jade masks. Jade earrings, 32 jade pearls, and more than 8,000 natural pearls were also found. Most of the stele uncovered here are so weathered that they can now no longer be deciphered, but a few still testify to richly decorated personalities and calendar dates.

Calakmul receives few visitors. Those who do come have the place more or less to themselves and can wander through the settlement admiring an exotic selection of animals and plants. You should plan to spend at least two nights at the eco-village in order to visit Calakmul, Chicanná, and Becán. The night sky over the jungle is also spectacular. Looking up from the terrace of our room

1−2 The Mayan city of Becan in the jungle of Campeche is surrounded by a five-meter-deep (16 feet) ditch around the main pyramid. It is famous for its palaces and underground walks.
3 The "Great Acropolis" in the Mayan City of Edzná in the north of Campeche.
4−5 In Chicanná, in the House of the Serpent Mouth, the stylized motifs on the façades are particularly impressive.

1 – 2 Campeche Cathedral, seen from the Casa Vieja restaurant on the zócalo. A small flight of stairs leads up to the terrace.
3 In the old town of Campeche: the street to Puerta del Mar.
4 Taking a well-earned break: Rosendo Tuyu, a descendent of the Maya, works in the Hacienda Uayamón.

we see countless shooting stars whilst listening to the secret sounds of the jungle.

Our route takes us on to Kohunlich via Xpuhil. We arrive dusty, sweaty, and disheveled, having been given a good shaking by the countless potholes in the road. And then? We find ourselves standing in a spacious, elegant lobby in the middle of the jungle. We look out over a huge "infinity pool" and over a jungle with the tallest palm trees we have ever seen. Herbal aromas waft out of the wellness center and an older couple is sitting in the lobby savoring a richly decorated exotic cocktail. We are in the legendary Explorean Kohunlich, a luxury resort with 40 Mayan-style bungalows operated here by the Mexican hotel group Posadas, just under two kilometers (1.25 miles) away from the actual Mayan site itself.

We rent a bicycle and make our way to the pyramids. Deafening shrieks from the jungle set my pulse racing: are there pumas here, I ask myself? – remembering the pair of jungle cats that caused some excitement when they turned up in the Mayan city of Palenque some years ago. My girlfriend has an explanation at the ready: "That's bound to be a tape recording." I'm not so sure: Mexicans are very innovative and like to come up with new ideas for entertaining the tourists – but jungle sounds on tape? Surely not! I enter the site with some trepidation.

A group of tourists standing some distance away sees us and waves. What can it all mean? Should we go or come over? We pluck up the courage and walk over and find the elderly couple we had seen in the hotel lobby, accompanied by a tour guide kitted out in a tropical-adventure look who gestures up into the treetops. That's where all the noise is coming from. A family of howling monkeys is ensconced up there and father is making all the noise to protect the wife and kids from us predators.

The name Kohunlich is not Mayan but derives from the English words "cohune" (oil lamp) and "ridge." The site was discovered in 1912 by the American archeologist Raymond Merwin and registered under the name "Clarksville." Mexican archeologists only began excavating in the 1960s. The site is small – it measures only 2 square kilometers (0.8 square miles). Many buildings are still covered by the jungle. We now know that Kohunlich belongs to the Classic to Late Classic Mayan period (250 to 900 AD). The Pyramid of the Masks, built in the Petén style, is its most impressive building. The two-meter (7 feet) masks are decorated with earrings and serpents, symbolizing the sun god Kinich Ahau. Kohunlich is fascinating, above all, because of its unique situation in the middle of the jungle. When the howling monkeys stop their commotion, a mysterious stillness descends over the site and only the wind rustles through the mighty palm trees.

Chetumal is the capital of the state of Quinta Roo. It is not a tourist attraction but deserves a visit nonetheless: the Museo de las Culturas Mayas (Museum of Mayan Cultures) is the best of its kind. Information is presented interactively on Mayan culture, its visions, its knowledge of the universe, and its development up to and including the present day. The section on Mayan astrological

1 Traditional Mayan architecture: the palm roof over the open restaurant in the Explorean Kohunilch creates a pleasant atmosphere.
2 A clear view from the terrace into the depths of the jungle and the Mayan site Kohunlich.
3 Luxury in the jungle: suite in the Explorean Kohunlich.

expertise, on their knowledge of tides, their use of numbers, and on their script is particularly interesting. They were able to calculate the orbit of the planet Venus with almost complete accuracy (0.08 days) and predict eclipses of the sun and moon. Using interactive installations, visitors can discover how the Maya calculated their calendars and even work out their own date of birth in Mayan numerals. Replicas of stele and codices, including the famous Dresden codex, are also on show,.

Laguna Bacalar – just under 50 kilometers (31 miles) long and about two kilometers (1.25 miles) wide – is only a few kilometers away from Chetumal in the direction of Tulum. It is famous for its different-colored water and is also known as the Laguna de los Siete Colores. The town of the same name and San Felipe fortress seem untouched by modern civilization, despite their proximity to the long-distance Chetumal–Cancún highway. Rich citizens from Chetumal have built some elegant holiday homes on the banks of the lagoon. There is a pool and a water sports club, but no hotels of note have yet been constructed. The lovingly restored San Felipe fortress gives visitors an indication of the former significance of

Bacalar (in Mayan, Bac'Halal: "place of reeds"). The town rises majestically from the lagoon banks. When the Spaniards arrived here, it was all over for the Maya. They were conquered and expelled and Gaspar Pacheco founded a town here that he called Villa Salamanca de Bacalar. In contrast to their successes in other regions, however, the new arrivals did not prosper straightaway.

The Spaniards did not really exploit Bacalar's geographical situation until the 17th century. Once they had found out how to make use of Bacalar's ocean connection (the lagoon flows into the Río Hondo via the Chac River and then on into the Bay of Chetumal through a network of shallow channels), the town became an important trading center from which the valuable log-wood and rubber were transported to Spain. Naturally, the town's prosperity made it a magnet for English and Dutch pirates and the Spaniards soon began constructing fortifications.

The view from the crenellated walls over the lagoon is spectacular. The water shimmers in all shades of emerald green, turquoise, and night blue. The fortress museum provides interesting and entertaining insights into the region's Spanish history.

Campeche, Calakmul, Kohunlich, and Bacalar

Getting there and when to travel
Air: from Mexico City to Chetumal or via Cancún.
Bus: regular overland bus service several times a day from Cancún or Campeche to Chetumal.
Car: from Campeche to Chicanná (Calakmul) via Champotón and Francisco Escárcega. From Chicanná on to Becán, Xpuhil, and Kohunlich to Chetumal or from Cancún via Tulum.
Best travel time: November to May.

Where to stay
****Hacienda Uayamón*. Tel: 981/829 75 27, fax: 923 79 63, e-mail: reservations1@thehaciendas.com, www.haciendas-mexico.com/uayamon/overview.php
****Hacienda Blanca Flor*. Tel: 999/925 80 42, fax: 925 91 11 (Mérida), e-mail: hblancaf@prodigy.net.mx
****Hotel Plaza Campeche*. Comfortable business hotel on the edge of the old town, Calle 10, No. 126A. Tel: 981/811 90 00, e-mail: hotelplazacampeche@hotmail.com, www.hotelplazacampeche.com
****Chicanná Ecovillage*. An ecologically-run, lovely hotel built on stilts. Two-storey rustic bungalows on the edge of Calakmul's biosphere reserve. Tel: 983/871 60 75, fax: 871 60 74, e-mail: chicanna@campeche.sureste.com, www.hotelmex.net
*****Explorean Kohunlich*, Dream resort set in the middle of the jungle on a little country road that turns off to the right just before Chetumal. Trips/guided tours of the pyramids, kayak tours on rivers and lagoons such as Chacambacan or Huay-Pix, moutainbike tours and night rambles through the jungle. Tel: 55/53 26 69 00, fax: 53 26 60 00 (central reservation office in Mexico City). Local telephone in Kohunlich: 972/894 11 73, in Europe: 00 49-69/66 41 96 40, e-mail: reserv@fiestaamericana.com.mx, www.theexplorean.com.mx/posadas
****Hotel Holiday Inn Chetumal*, Av. Héroes No. 171A, center. Unspectacular exterior but with a beautiful garden and pool. Small, but very well appointed rooms. Fantastic breakfast buffet. Tel: 983/835 04 00, fax: 835 04 29, e-mail: ventaschtmhi@holidayinnchetumal.com.mx, www.holiday-inn.com/chetumalmex, www.holidayinnmaya.com.mx

Must See
Bacalar Lagoon: discover the remote corners of the lagoon once used by pirates. Motorized dinghies or small sailing boats available. Swimming opportunities in the lagoon channels.
The "Cenote Azul" on the outskirts of Bacalar: surrounded by lush tropical forest, the dark blue, 90-meter-deep (295 feet) waters of the cenote are an excellent spot for swimming, diving, and snorkeling. Great view from the restaurant terrace.

Information
Campeche: Secretaría de Turismo, Av. Ruiz Cortines s/n, Plaza Moch-Couoh. Tel: 981/881 92 55, fax: 816 67 67, e-mail: turismo@campeche.gob.mx, www.campechetravel.com
Chetumal: Secretaría de Turismo de Quintana Roo, Fid′ -miso de Promoción Turísica, De la Grand Costa Maya, 22 de Enero, s/n. Tel: 983/832 66 47, fax: 832 51 30, e-m promocion@grandcostamaya.com, sedetur.qroo.go .mx Blvd. Belisario Domínguez 950, Tuxtla Gutiérrez, toli ree domestic calls 01-80 02 80/35 00, e-mail: turismo@chiapas.gob.mx, www.chiapas.turista.co .

The Wild North

The Most Beautiful Stretch of Railway in the World
Visiting with the Rarámuri Indians in Copper Canyon

Our journey with the legendary "Chepe" – as the Chihuahua al Pacífico is known – takes us from Los Mochis on the Pacific coast through the wild Sierra Tarahumara to Chihuahua in the north.

It is uncomfortably cool in the early morning hours at Los Mochis station. The town is still asleep. But there is plenty of hustle and bustle in the railway station. Tourists from all over the world, especially backpackers, and locals wrapped in thick ponchos stand around shivering and waiting for the signal to get in the train. I was thankful that the hotel had provided us early risers with coffee and biscuits – there certainly wasn't anything in the way of a cup of coffee or a sandwich to be bought here.

The doors finally open just before six and we are allowed into the legendary "Chepe." Late sleepers who miss this train or those unable to purchase a ticket have a long wait ahead of them and should bring something to eat and drink to tide them over. The train starts one hour later. There is no restaurant on board. The "Primera Express" makes only 15 stops on its way to Chihuahua but the second-class train stops up to 65 times – every time somebody wants to get on or off. It is long past midnight by the time the train rolls into Chihuahua. If there is one stretch of railroad that deserves the superlative "most beautiful in the world," then it's this one. The 15-hour journey covers 653 kilometers (405 miles), climbs 2,500 meters (8,200 feet), crosses 39 bridges at mind-boggling heights, and passes through 89 tunnels. The massive mountains of the Sierra are home to historic mining towns and the villages of the mysterious Rarámuri Indians, also known as Tarahumara by the Mexicans.

The powerful diesel locomotive pulls us gently out into the morning. In the light of the rising sun, the dry plain with its cacti looks like a landscape from a Sergio Leone western. Shortly after nine o'clock we have completed the first stage of our journey, arriving at the enchanting colonial city of El Fuerte, which lies at a height of 1,200 meters (4,940 feet). The town's name is derived

1 Bigger than the Rocky Mountains: the copper canyons in North Mexico.
2 Rarámuri Indian.
3 "Chepe," the legendary "Chihuahua al Pacifico" on its way from Los Mochis to Chihuahua.
4 After hours on the train, arriving at Divisadero: fantastic view onto the Sierra Madre.

1 Panorama at Divisadero.
2 Waiting for the train in the Sierra Tarahumara.
3 – 4 In the course of its 653 kilometer (405 miles) journey, the "Chepe" train climbs 2,500 meters (8,200), crosses 39 bridges, and passes through 89 tunnels.
5 The conductor greets his guests personally.
6 Compartment with a view: standing-room only for looking and enjoying.

from a fortress that the Spanish once built here as a fortification against recalcitrant Indians, and for the protection of the silver treasures that came from the mines of the Sierra Madre.

El Fuerte is one of the most interesting towns in the north of Mexico: it was founded as La Villa de San Juan de Carapoa in 1564. The first Jesuits and Franciscan monks arrived here towards the end of the 16th century. The town was an important watering hole for Spanish colonial masters on their way to Arizona and California and developed into a trade center on the "Royal Silver Route." By road, the trip from Los Mochis to El Fuerte takes around 90 minutes and provides an alternative starting point for those who would rather catch the train here at 9 o'clock. But there is another

reason to take the train from El Fuerte: the Hotel Posada del Hidalgo. It is said that Zorro – the legendary Mexican Robin Hood – once lived in the grand colonial mansion. Today, it is an unbelievably beautiful luxury hotel with a splendid, lush garden.

El Fuerte marks the starting point of one of the great technical marvels of the 20th century: the slow ascent of the railroad stretch covered by the Ferrocarril de Chihuahua al Pacífico into the wild Sierra Tarahumara. Narrow, fissured rock faces alternate with picturesque valleys covered with tropical plants and trees. The train sways over bridges at vertiginous heights with spectacular views into the depths onto babbling streams and little farmsteads – and the odd freight carriage that has gone off the rails. We stand on the train platform and let the wind rush into our faces, taking one photo after the other.

We owe all of this to the vision of one enterprising businessman: in 1861, the American Albert Kinsey Owen wanted to build a railroad from Topolobampo near Los Mochis to Kansas City, which would have shortened the existing route from San Francisco to Kansas City by 400 miles. The Mexican government gave Owen permission to go ahead two years later but then his money dried up and the contract was passed on to Foster Higgins of the Río Grande, Sierra Madre & Pacific Railway Company.

Higgins managed to complete the stretch of railroad from Ciudad Juárez on the border with Texas, north of Chihuahua, to Casas Grandes – and then he, too, gave up. Nearly 40 years passed before Enrique Creel of the Kansas City, Mexico & Orient Railway took up the project and completed the stretch of railroad as far as La Junta between 1910 and 1914. During that time, Creel also began to build a railway from Ojinaga via Chihuahua to the station named Creel, for its creator, in the heart of the Sierra Tarahumara. This time it was the Mexican Revolution that put paid to further ambitious plans and it was 1928 before the stretch between Topolobampo and El Fuerte was completed. But it was only in the year 1940, almost a century after Albert Kinsey Owen was first decried as a dreamer and utopist and after the nationalization of the railways, that the Mexican government filled the last great gap from El Fuerte to Creel – a masterpiece of engineering and final proof that Owen was not a utopist but a visionary.

The construction of the railway line through the imposing Sierra marked the beginning of the constant tightrope walk performed by the local Rarámuri Indians between tradition and progress. The Rarámuri populated the north of Mexico long before the arrival of the Spanish conquistadors and missionaries. They are of Mongolian origin and came to Mexico via the Behring Strait over 20,000 years ago as hunters and gatherers and settled on the American continent as hunters. Driven out from their fertile lands and forest hunting grounds by the Spanish colonial masters and later by wealthy landowners, they retreated into the inaccessible canyons and lived from farming, raising cattle, and hunting – a way of life that the 50,000 or so surviving Rarámuri still practice today in an area that is larger than the Rocky Mountains. Together with the Huicholes from Jalisco and Nayarit and the Yaquís from Sinaloa, the Rarámuri are considered the oldest of Mexico's indigenous tribes.

Quite a few Rarámuri still live in caves in conditions that the average European finds quite inconceivable. What appears picturesque at first glance is, in fact, a way of life characterized by deprivation and sickness. Health care is minimal. Without the support of religious-based and private aid organizations, they would hardly be able to survive. Most of the Rarámuri, however, live within extended families in wood-and-clay huts grouped together in hamlets called rancherías and surrounded by apple, plum, and peach trees. They cultivate corn, beans, and squash. The rancherías are loosely organized in communities (comunidades)

presided over by a governor who is democratically elected by both men and women. In late spring, after the end of the dry period and before the beginning of the agrarian cycle when food is scarce, many Rarámuri eat seeds and roots, rodents, and the larvae of a butterfly native to the region and known to be particularly rich in vitamin C.

Rarámuri mythology is a mixture of pre-Spanish and Christian elements. The traditional running competitions that take place several times a year are an important part of their spiritual life.

1 Approximately 50,000 Rarámuri Indians still live in small villages in the gorges of the Sierra Tarahumara.
2 Rarámuri couple in typical costume; the hotel Barrancas Mirador in the background.
3 The young Rarámuri carry on the old traditions.
4 Rarámuri Indian woman in the Barranca del Cobre; tourism has become an important source of income.
5 Between tradition and modernity: Tarahumara in Batopilas.
6 Painting in the Hotel Barrancas Mirador.

These competitions last for several days and nights and can involve distances of over 200 kilometers (124 miles). The runner often kicks an orange-sized, wooden ball in front of him. The Rarámuri are also known as Tarahumara — which means "foot runner" in their language. It is no coincidence that quite a few of Mexico's Olympic runners are descended from the Rarámuri. Night runners have their way lit by torches carried by fellow competitors. A festival involving the consumption of large amounts of tesgüino, or corn beer, accompanies each race. Mutual respect for their fellow men and women is an important aspect of Rarámuri culture. Even larger assemblies are characterized by handshakes between all those present – including the tourists.

The traditional costume worn by the men comprises short, white breeches held at the waist by a colorful sash, and wide-sleeved shirts. They often wind scarves around their heads. Women mostly wear colorful, cotton skirts – red being the color of choice – blouses, and colored headscarves. They carry their children – and other loads – in large shawls that they drape around their bodies. Rarámuri children are encouraged to become independent at an early age and are treated as adults by the time they are 14 or 15. As a whole, the Rarámuri are excellent craftsmen, creating masterpieces as potters, weavers, and basket makers.

When we stop at Divisadero station for 15 minutes to enjoy the breathtaking view onto the grandiose canyon landscape, a group of mainly younger Rarámuri women rush onto the train: chattering away, laughing, and quite enchanting to look at in their colorful

1–2 Views onto Copper Canyon in the evening light from the balcony of the Hotel Barrancas Mirador.
3 As if it were part of the cliffs: the Hotel Barrancas Mirador on the edge of the copper gorges.
4 Expert walkers can go down from here to the Urique River through several climate zones and fascinating contrasts from fresh mountain air to tropical heat.

skirts and headscarves, they offer baskets and skillfully woven belts for sale, whilst their men stand on the quay in cowboy boots and hats with their identically dressed sons and wait for business to be concluded.

In the late afternoon we reach Creel, the center of the Sierra Tarahumara. Until a few years ago, it was just a small place with unpaved roads. Today, it feels like a modern town with restaurants and several hotels in all price categories. For some years now, Creel has been part of a network of highways connecting it to Chihuahua, Parral, and Los Mochis – an area that is also popular

with cyclists. Four-wheeled motorbikes stand around here in place of horses, as well as jeeps and vans for tourist excursions into the countryside.

A big surprise awaits us in the Posada Barrancas Mirador. The Balderrama hotel group has created an architectural jewel not far from the highest point on Copper Canyon: two elongated buildings hang like birds' nests from the cliffs. Each room has a spacious balcony with a breathtaking view over the canyon. It smells of wood and pines, the air is clear, and the surrounding mountains seem within touching distance.

Divisadero and Creel are the best points of departure for tours to the Tarahumara villages, the little Sierra missions, and the immense gorges – either on foot or on the back of a donkey or horse as far as the Urique River. The descent is characterized by unbelievable contrasts, with vegetation that changes every 100 meters (130 feet) or so and ends up as a tropical forest on the canyon floor. It's

1 Adventure stories await visitors in the Museo Mirador in El Fuerte.
2 Catch a glimpse of how the legendary Zorro lived in the Posada del Hidalgo.
3 Important trade center and transit stop on the way to the United States: El Fuerte. The splendid palaces from colonial times testify to the wealth formerly accumulated by the silver barons.
4–6 Restaurant and patio of the Posada del Hidalgo.

particularly spectacular in the winter: snow at the top and tropical heat and lush verdure at the bottom. I'm not a particularly good walker so we arrange to be driven to the legendary mining town of Batopilas along winding roads that take us down into one of the Sierra's deepest gorges. Batopilas, situated 460 meters (1510 feet) above sea level on the river of the same name, was famous for its colonial beauty and its luxurious gardens and plantations that earned it the epithet "treasure of the Sierra Madre." Despite its great prosperity, it looked for a while as though it might end up as a ghost town. The town was founded in 1708, but only became important with the exploitation of the silver mines at the end of the 18th century. The American Alexander R. Shepherd, a former mayor of Washington D.C., accumulated immense wealth here: his "Batopilas Mining Company" was one of the largest in the world.

Pancho Villa and his gang once managed to pull off an incredible stunt during the revolution when they robbed him of a huge load of silver bars worth an incredible 40,000 US dollars. Shepherd brought great technological progress and a diverse cultural life to the town. He died in 1902 and bequeathed his mines to one of his sons, who continued exploiting them until 1920 and then gave up. Others came after him and searched in vain for new silver veins,

and Batopilas was eventually forgotten. Today, the city's wealth and fame are based on the tourist industry. The stretch between Creel and Chihuahua is not as spectacular – although the area around Cuauhtémoc is interesting because of its large Mennonite community. We decide to return to Los Mochis. The light conditions are different on the way back – and we can enjoy it all over again from a different perspective.

Copper Canyon – the world's most beautiful railway line

Getting there and when to travel
Air: from Mexico City to Chihuahua with Aeroméxico, from Mexico City and Guadalajara to Los Mochis with Aerocalifornia.
Bus: from Mazatlán to Los Mochis and El Fuerte and on by train. Very good road network in the Sierra Tarahumara. Ferry service between La Paz and the port of Topolobampo.
Best travel time: April, May, June.

Where to stay
*****Posada Barrancas Mirador*, luxury hotel with 52 rooms directly on Copper Canyon. Tel: 635/818 70 46, fax: 812 00 46, e-mail: hotelsbal@mexicoscoppercanyon.com, www.mexicoscoppercanyon.com/mirador.htm

*****Posada Hidalgo El Fuerte*, 12 lovely rooms furnished with antiques, pool, wellness center, splendid garden.
Tel: 698/893 02 42, fax: 893 11 94,
e-mail: infor@hotelposadadelhidalgo.com
www.mexicoscoppercanyon.com/posadahidalgo.htm

Must See
Easter week in the Sierra Tarahumara. The Rarámuris meet in the missions in order to celebrate a mixture of Christian and heathen rites centered on the crucifixion and resurrection of Christ. A colorful spectacle. Early hotel and train reservation recommended.

Local Attractions
Mission Cuzárare, 21 km (13 miles) to the south of Creel: inhabited and uninhabited caves decorated with Indian drawings in the vicinity.
Waterfalls at Basaseáchic: with a drop height of approx. 300 meters (985 feet), the highest in Mexico. Close to a beautiful lake.
Divisadero Station: spectacular view onto the Copper, Urique, and Tararécura canyons. Rarámuri arts and crafts market.
Cerocahui: working mission schools founded in the 17th century by Jesuits, 12 km (7 miles) to Bahuichivo station.

Information
Ferrocarril Mexicano (Ferromex): Calle Méndez y 24 a, Chihuahua. Tel: 614/439 72 10, 439 72 12, fax: 521/439 72 08, e-mail: chepe@ferromex.com.mx, www.chepe.com.mx
Tourism Ministry Chihuahua, Libertad 1300, 1er Piso, Edif. Agustin Melgar, Chihuahua. Tel: 614/429 34 12, fax: 429 33 20, www.chihuahua.gob.mx/turismoweb
Tourism offices in the town halls at Los Mochis, El Fuerte, and Batopilas.

Snorkeling, Golf, and Going Out
Cabo San Lucas, San José del Cabo, and La Paz

Both Cabos – Cabo San Lucas and San José del Cabo – now better known as the tourist corridor "Los Cabos" – are situated on the southern tip of the peninsular of Baja California. Here, where the Pacific meets the Sea of Cortéz, visitors can look forward to a holiday paradise rich in natural contrasts with unique sporting opportunities: diving, snorkeling, sailing, windsurfing, golfing, bathing – visitors are spoilt for choice.

The entire stretch of beach, 33 kilometers (20 miles) from Cabo San Lucas to San José del Cabo, is occupied by large, elegant hotel complexes that nestle snugly around golf courses with their carefully manicured greens, their little lagoons, and rivers that contrast so dramatically with the impressive mountain panorama and the barren desert. Before them lie white beaches and sapphire-blue seas. out of which strange and craggy rock formations arise. Cabo San Lucas is smart and lively with its own quay at which expensive American yachts rock gently alongside sport-fishing vessels and excursion boats. Cabo San Lucas is regarded as the El Dorado for keen anglers. There are huge stocks of marlin, sailfish, seabream, and tuna in the Sea of Cortéz. Famous amateur anglers such as John Wayne or the singer Bing Crosby played their part in turning the former fishing village Cabo San Lucas into a world-famous holiday resort. The Hotel Palmilla and the fortress-style Westin Regina Resort, built by the famous architect Juan Sordo Madaleno to occupy a whole hill overlooking the sea, are two of the top hotels.

San José del Cabo, by contrast, is quiet and picturesque. Although it is not situated directly on the coast, its cheerfully painted houses make for a wonderfully romantic atmosphere. The Hotel Casa Natalia on the Plaza San José – a boutique hotel that belongs to the group of "Small Luxury Hotels of the World" – is a perfect base from which to discover the small town and wander through its galleries and arts and crafts shops. The Hotel Palmilla is famous for its legendary gardens. It was one of the first hotels to be built

1 Holiday fun: Debbie and Timber in Playa Medano near Cabo San Lucas.
2 Tradition and progress: mariachi in front of the cool building of the Hotel Westin Regina in Los Cabos.
3 Fascinating contrasts on the Bahía de Cortéz.
4 Land's End: the southern tip of Baja California.

here decades ago, about three kilometers (2 miles) from San José del Cabo on the way to Cabo San Lucas. In the early years, access was possible only by ship or by plane. The crème de la crème of the Mexican and American jet set still meets up here. The Palmilla golf club was designed by the famous golf course architect Jack Nicklaus.

Los Cabos is home to the PGA Senior Slam, remunerated with several hundred thousand dollars. Golf courses such as Cabo del Sol, with a spectacular view over the coastline, and El Dorado (also designed by Jack Nicklaus), which stretches along the coast and into the gorges and valleys of the interior, as well as Cabo Real (designed by Robert Trent Jones II) or the Cabo San Lucas Country Club (Roy and Matt Dye) enjoy world repute.

Early next morning, we make our way to Cabo San Lucas, to take a boat, along with other tourists, to the famous rock arch El Arco. The going is pretty rough here where the Pacific Ocean and the Sea of Cor éz meet and mighty waves crash onto the rocks. The boat has a glass floor through which we can observe the colorful

1 Calm, crystal-clear water: taking the kayak out to see the sea lions on Espiritu Santo Island near La Paz.
2 Paddle, paddle, paddle … we're nearly there.
3 The 18th-century Jesuit mission of San Ignacio, on the way from Santa Rosalia to Guerrero Negro.
4 Hot, dry, yet fascinating: the Desierto Central Nature Park near Catavina.

sea life. These are great diving grounds. The numerous diving outfitters also offer trips to the wrecks of pirate ships that once went down in stormy seas. Now, they constitute a unique biosphere for innumerable fish in all the colors of the rainbow.

The nightlife in Cabo San Lucas is a real challenge. There is something for everybody here: from ultra modern discos frequented for the most part by young American teenagers shaking it down to earsplitting rhythms and flashing spotlights, to sleazy striptease clubs and on to elegant restaurants and cozy bars – such as the Bar Pancho, which serves 250 different kinds of tequila. For some peace and quiet, just turn around and head back to the comfort of San José del Cabo.

An interesting route takes us on to La Paz. Despite the growth in tourism, the port town and capital of Baja California Sur was able to maintain its typically Mexican character. Walking along under the palm trees on the pretty beach promenade Malecón in the evening, you'll find yourself rubbing shoulders with the locals, also out to enjoy some after-work relaxation and a view onto the splendid sunset. Real life does not begin here until the late afternoon – it's just too hot during the day, especially in the summer months. The nearby harbor of Pichilingüe is the terminal for ferries from Los Mochis, Mazatlán, and Puerto Vallarta that disgorge whole caravans of cars and lorries onto the southern Baja. La Paz means "peace," but the history of the city has been anything but peaceful. Mexico's conqueror, Hernán Cortés himself, founded a settlement in the bay. Like so many others who came after him, the inhospitable conditions here forced him to concede defeat. In the 16th century, famous pirates such as Francis Drake and Thomas Cavendish came to the bay, intent on robbing the richly laden Philippine trade ships. It was only later that the Spaniards

began to fortify the Californian ports. Even Captain Sebastian Vizcaíno, who traveled all the way from Acapulco on a special mission in search of pearls, had to give up. Only the Jesuits, who founded their first mission here about 100 years later, managed to pacify the Indians. After the Mexican-American War (1847–1848) and a brief period of occupation by an American named William Walker, who wanted to found his own state here, the town finally began to live up to its name.

La Paz is an ideal point of departure for fishing tours on the sea or trips to the Island of Espíritu Santo – a large, rocky island inhabited by sea lions. A speedboat takes us far out into the sea, bouncing off the waves for what seems like an interminable trip. But the smell of fish – and rotting fish – tells us that we are close to our destination. First we see only a few, then a few more and it is not long before we are surrounded by hordes of sea lions. We transfer to kayaks and paddle round the island. The seals are so audacious that they come up close and push their noses against the boats, inviting us to play with them in the water. Some of the other visitors leave their kayaks on the beach and join the seals for some fun and games. At one stage, a group of Japanese investors planned to turn the island into a hotel resort. Happily, a group of local

environmentalists protested and the plans were dropped. La Paz has many nice little restaurants on Malecón and its side streets that serve everything from pizza to steak, seafood and fish, even burgers. Those that don't make it into the mountains to admire the legendary cliff paintings by the indigenous population can admire replicas in the Anthropological Museum.

The best place to stay is the beautiful hotel La Casa Azul, opened here by Esther Ammann in an 18th-century colonial palace (now a protected monument) in 1999. The Swiss globetrotter first came to Baja California in 1995 to do some surfing and fell in love with the town. It was her dream to create a Bed & Breakfast here and she devoted great energy to the individual design of the rooms – and even the lush garden bears her stamp. The best beaches are situated to the north of the town, going towards Pichilingüe. Coves with crystal-clear water and fine sand are perfect for snorkeling. But beware: there is no natural shade on Pichilingüe beach: no palms, just arid mountain landscape and the omnipresent cacti. But there are plenty of good beach restaurants where one can take cover from the sun – and enjoy excellent fish dishes. Puerto Balandra, with its mushroom-shaped rocks, and Playa Coromel also have good beaches.

Cabo San Lucas, San José del Cabo, and La Paz – Snorkeling, Golfing, and Going Out

Getting there and when to travel
Air: from Mexico City to La Paz, San Juan del Cabo or Cabo San Lucas. International flights directly from US cities such as San Diego or Los Angeles.
Ferry: from Los Mochis (Topolobampo), Mazatlán, and Puerto Vallarta.
Car: the Mex 1 highway covers the entire peninsular from Tijuana and Ensenada on the American border to La Paz and Cabo San Lucas in the south. Comfortable bus service to and from all major towns.

Where to stay
San José del Cabo: *****Hotel Casa Natalia*, 18 finely furnished rooms. Boulevard Mijares No 4, San José del Cabo 23400. Tel. and fax: 624/142 51 00, fax: 624/142 51 10, e-mail: mexicoquestions@casanatalia.com, www.casanatalia.com
La Paz: ****El Angel Azul*, Bed & Breakfast Hotel, Independencia 518 esq/Guillermo Prieto, Centro, 23000 La Paz, Baja California Sur, Mexico. Tel: 125 51 30, e-mail: hotel@elangelazul.com, www.elangelazul.com

Must See
Carnival in La Paz, famous for its colorful processions.
The Diving and Kayak School Boa in La Paz (for kayaks, located at the end of Malecón to the north behind the Hotel El Moro. Tel: 612/125 56 36) and Funbaja Adventure, tel: 612/121 58 84 organize tours to the most beautiful diving and snorkeling grounds.

Local Attractions
Espíritu Santo, La Partida and Islotes islands with their seal colonies and many different kinds of birds.
Mission Estero de las Palmas, founded in 1730 with its beautiful little church. A mosaic on the façade commemorates the murder of Father Nicolás Tamarl, one of the mission's founders, at the hands of Indians.

Information
Los Cabos Tourism Trust (FITURCA), Fidelcomiso de Turismo de Los Cabos, Lazaro Cardenas Edificio Posada, s/n, Colonia el Medano, Cabo San Lucas, Baja California Sur, CP 23410 Mexico. Tel: 624/143 47 77, www.visitloscabos.org
There is no official tourist information center in La Paz. Information under www.gbcs.gob.mx

1 Pool and beach at the "Twin Dolphin Resort" in Cabo San Lucas.
2 For gourmets: "Damiana" restaurant in San José del Cabo.
3-4 Pool and a room in the "Casa Natalia", San José del Cabo.
5 The best seafood for miles is served here in Mariscos Mazatlán in Cabo San Lucas.

Contrasts on the Baja California
From the Artists' City of Todos Santos to the Cactus Forests

The gigantic Cardon cactus and other succulents stretch out their thorns towards us. There seems to be very little here, in the center of the peninsular Baja California, that encourages human life. Nonetheless, this wilderness is both unapproachable and attractive.

The Spanish conquistadors christened this country "Calida Fornax" – "hot oven." And that is true of the Baja California in every sense. Only the toughest of plants survives the long periods of drought. But as soon as a few raindrops fall, the landscape is transformed into a sea of colorful blossoms. And then it is easy to believe that 2,500 plant species live here.

It is the contrasts that exist here, side by side on a peninsular that is 1,250 kilometers (775 miles) long and an average of 90 kilometers (56 miles) wide, that make the region so popular: cacti on high mountains, deep canyons, deserts, palm oases, wide beaches with fantastic rock formations, and an unparalleled diversity of flora and fauna. The Baja California is one of the most thinly populated areas in the world. It is divided into two states – Baja California Norte and Baja California Sur. It is the south that attracts the tourists although the development of the region to this end did not begin until 1974, with the construction of the Carretera Transpeninsular from Tijuana to Cabo San Lucas. The old mission towns and fishing villages suddenly became attractive holiday resorts.

We are heading for Todos Santos – or All Souls. The trip from La Paz, the lively capital of Baja California Sur, is an adventure in itself. We take National Highway no. 19 for about 70 kilometers (12 for about 43 miles), traveling southeast along the Sierra de San Lázaro through beautiful landscapes in which deserts full of cacti exist side by side with mountains and palm oases.

Founded in 1724 as a mission at the foot of the Sierra de la Laguna, Todos Santos was just a hideaway for hippies until the 1970s. Today, it is a popular meeting place for artists and is equipped with all the requisite institutions: numerous galleries, exquisite restaurants, and beautiful hotels. It is remarkably green; the area is fertile. Sugar cane used to be the main cash crop but

1 Inspirational artists' city: Todos Santos.
2 Just a few raindrops will transform a cactus desert into a sea of flowers.
3 Dream on: the Hotel Posada la Poza in Todos Santos.
4 In the Canyon de la Zorra, Sierra de la Laguna.

1 Hotel Ventana Bay Resort to the south of La Paz: an insider tip for sports enthusiasts.
2–3 Natural paradise without TV and seawater instead of chlorine in the pool: the Posada la Poza.
4 Stylish: the El Gusto restaurant in the Posada la Poza – dream views and exquisite cuisine.

today the locals live mainly from cultivating chilis, mangos, avocados, and papayas – and tourism, of course. With its colonial architecture and its luxurious gardens, the town is considered the jewel of the Baja California Sur. The Casa de la Cultura and the Teatro General Manuel Márquez de León are particularly worthwhile visiting.

People often say that the town's popularity derives from the Eagles' song "Hotel California" that brought thousands of fans here to the peaceful village. There really is a "Hotel California" here but it has nothing to do with the fictive house in the song. That was built much later.

We are tempted by the Posada la Poza, a delightful little hotel situated two kilometers (1,25 miles) outside the town. A Swiss couple (he's a former banker and she's an artist of Czech descent)

built their dream here: a boutique hotel set in a splendid garden. The seven spacious rooms are cozy and decorated with paintings by the owner-artist. Sitting on the Ballena deck enjoying a margarita, we feel as though we have landed in paradise. Tempting aromas from the kitchen draw us into the hotel restaurant El Gusto.

For our first glimpse of local vegetation, we decide to go for a late afternoon walk through the cactus forests. Walking in the heat of the day is torture. "You must wear good shoes and long trousers," Juan tells us. We soon find out that he's right. It's easy to stumble over the cactus roots or thorny thistles – and then there are the animals. Scorpions lurk under stones, and now and then we hear snakes hissing.

120 different species of cactus grow here in Baja California. Fifty of these are endemic and grow only here. The Cardon cacti attain a height of 20 meters (66 feet), reaching up into the sky like giant candelabras – the biggest cacti in South America. The best time to enjoy the cactus forests is from August to October, when cacti and succulents are in flower and the place is "just crawling with botanists," according to Juan. We enjoy the light of the setting sun

that turns the cactus desert into a ghost forest. Above us, the stars spread themselves over a spectacular night sky.

Once we are back in Todos Santos, we abandon ourselves to the pleasures of the lively local nightlife. A mixed bag of guests populates the bars and restaurants: tourists, intellectuals, artists, and hippies … We start our tour in the Café Santa Fe, the town's most famous restaurant, and go on to the famous ice-cream parlor Nevería Rocce. From there, we move on to the jazz night at the Café Brown and end up in the La Copa Wine Bar for one last drink. But we haven't spotted any celebrities: we should have come in February, when the annual art festival draws more prominent crowds.

The next morning is set aside for some sun and sea: Todos Santos boasts some fantastic white beaches that overlook crystal-clear waters. The winds are constant and have made this region a paradise for surfers and kite surfers riding waves that are up to 15 meters (50 feet) high. The colorful sails skim across the water and through the air all day long. Surf meets are held here on a regular basis.

Todos Santos – contrasts on the Baja California

Getting there and when to travel
Air: Todos Santos has its own airport. Flights from the United States are the best option: via Franfurt/Main-Los Angeles or San Diego, for example. There are also flights from Mexico City to La Paz, Cabo San Lucas or San José del Cabo.
Car: Highway no. 1 from Tijuana to La Paz and from there on Highway no. 9 to Todos Santos is the most impressive drive.

Where to stay
*****Posada La Poza*. The former beach hotel in Todos Santos now offers seven spacious, comfortable, and cozy rooms, an exquisite restaurant and a bar as well as a saltwater pool in a wonderful garden. Various activities available.
Tel: 612/145 04 00, fax: 145 04 53,
e-mail: lapoza@prodigy.net.mx, www.lapoza.com
****Ventana Bay Resort*. Small resort situated on Ventana Bay to the south of La Paz. "Mr. Bill" is a remarkable source of information for all those interested in nature and sports activities and knows his way around the surroundings. The

hotel offers many activities: surfing, mountain biking, diving, deep sea fishing or walking in the cactus forests. Comfortable rooms with sea view and bungalows with private patios.
Tel: 612/114 02 22, e-mail: mrbill@ventanabay.com

Must See
The tropical gardens in Todos Santos (between Hidalgo and Obregón) are a unique paradise for birds. The botanical gardens situated 6 km (4 miles) outside the city on Highway 19 are also worth visiting.

Local Attractions
The former mining towns of El Triunfo and San Antionio provide interesting insights into the history of mining on the Baja California. Coming from La Paz on Highway 9, take the exit just after San Pedro onto the Carretera Transpeninsular. El Triunfo is accessible from La Ventana Bay via a country road. Guided walks through the cactus forests and in the Sierra. Also: mountainbiking, trekking, excursions to Land's End, to the seal island Espíritu Santo, and, from December to April, whale-watching close to Puerto López Mateos and San Carlos.

Information
Mexican Tourist Information Office, Taunusanlage 21, 60325 Frankfurt.
Tel: 0049-69 25 35 09, fax: 25 37 55.
e-mail: germany@visitmexico.com, www.visitmexico.com

Giants of the Seas
Mulegé and the San Ignacio Lagoon

Every winter they start out on their long journey from Alaska to the warmer waters off the Baja California: the gray whales. This is where they mate and where their babies are born before they return to the north in March and April, some 15 to 16 months after they came down here. We visited the giants of the sea with the American tour organizer "Baja Expeditions" – an unforgettable experience.

The pretty little town of Mulegé, situated on the coast of the Bahía Concepción on the Gulf of California, is the starting point for our expedition. We have three days in which to relax in the wonderful, environmentally-friendly Orchard Vacation Village, to doze by the pool or walk along the beautiful beaches. Mulegé is situated on a river – and there's no better place for a promenade than under palm trees on an embankment.

Our expedition exceeds all expectations. We start out early in the morning in a bright yellow bus, specially equipped for rough conditions, with camping gear for a whole village tied onto the roof. We take the road to Santa Rosalia and San Ignacio, through imposing mountains into the sand desert with its impressive cacti situated on the edge of the Desierto de Vizcaíno National Park. We have driven about 200 kilometers (124 miles) by the time we reach the famous lagoon and have had time to get acquainted with our fellow passengers – scientists from the United States, as well as normal tourists like ourselves. John, the scientist, keeps the bus entertained with his knowledge of desert flora and fauna. We can't wait to get to the whales. We can see only a few from the coastline, spouting water into the air. In the meantime, the "genies" from Baja Expeditions have set up comfortable tents and invited us into the "dining-tent." We feel like pioneers on a discovery expedition.

According to current estimates, the gray whale population totals approximately 26,000. In December, the mammals leave their natural habitat in Alaska and the Bering Sea in order to mate in the Baja California. After 13 months, the baby whales are born here. In March, the 25-ton animals that measure up to 15 meters (49 feet)

1 Comfortable: the pelicans in La Paz.
2 Unusually gentle and friendly: gray whale in the San Ignacio Lagoon.
3 Seals on the Los Islotes rocks off La Paz.
4 Fascinating encounter between man and animals: curious gray whales approach the tourists.

1 This shark does not bite: getting acquainted with a whale shark near La Paz.
2 Expedition into the Sierra de San Francisco: camp-fire romanticism
3 Magical peace: cemetery near San Ignacio.
4 Colorful underwater world: snorkeling near the Los Islotes rocks off La Paz.
5 Paradise for nature lovers: the Orchard Vacation Village in Mulegé.

in length start the return journey – covering a distance of about 16,000 kilometers (9900 miles).

The next morning, we finally get out onto the water. We take a small boat into San Ignacio lagoon. It takes quite a while before we see some of the whales: just a few who swim out towards us and circle the boat or ride alongside it. But then, more and more come out to us. Huge creatures come closer and closer, rub their bodies against the hull, nudge the boat in high spirits and then dive down again. It's unbelievable. Some come so close that we can reach out and stroke them. The calves are particularly curious. One of them dives under the boat, pushes it gently upwards and then comes up again somewhere else – as if playing hide-and-seek. Their movement, as they rise up to exhale the air from their lungs, is languorously elegant. And then they dive downwards again and all

that is left to see is the shadow of a dark tail fin. Despite their enormous size, they are incredibly gentle.

Our tour guide explains that the animals love to be splashed with water. No sooner said than done! We almost capsize the boat as we all bend over to cup water in our hands, splashing around like a bunch of children in the pool. And as if they'd been waiting for us to oblige, the whales swim up and swarm around us: so many, that the water is quite dark. It is not easy taking photos – everything is on the move and too much excitement could end in an unexpected bath.

Whale tourism could be a problem for these sensitive animals: the lagoon offers few opportunities for escape. That is why whale-watching is undertaken only with trained specialists. UNESCO has declared parts of the Bahía Sebastián Vizcaíno that adjoin the calm breeding waters of the lagoons a World Nature Site. Boat traffic is restricted in some of the lagoons. The second large, gray-whale breeding, calving, and nurturing area is a little further to the south, in the Bahía Magdalena.

There's no doubt about it: we are smitten. If we'd had more time, we would have loved to go to the Sea of Cortéz to watch the blue whales. But every good thing must come to an end, sometime.

Mulegé and the San Ignacio Lagoon – giants of the seas

Getting there and when to travel
Air: from Mexico City or via San Diego to Loreto or Santa Rosalia. There is a landing strip in Mulegé that is used by smaller charter planes.
Car: Mex 1 Highway, from Tijuana to San Ignacio. Take a side road to Laguna San Ignacio. Or from La Paz on Mex 1 to San Ignacio.
Bus: there is a bus service to Mulegé from every larger city.
Ship: with the ferry from Guaymas in the state of Sonora to Santa Rosalia.
Best travel time: December to April.

Where to stay
*****Orchard Vacation Village*, Mulegé, B.C.S., Mexico.
Tel: 303 00, fax: 301 09. The hotel is a time-share resort and only accepts bookings for at least three nights,
e-mail: orchardvvv@prodigy.net-mx,
www.bajalife.com/orchard/map.htm
Baja Expeditions Inc., 2625 Garnet Ave. San Diego,
CA 92109. Tel: 001-858/581 33 11, fax: 585/581 65 42,
e-mail: travel@bajaex.com, www.bajaex.com

Must See
Gray whales in the Lagoons of San Ignacio, Ojo de Liebre, and Scammon. The Parque Nacional de la Ballena Gris (about 3 km/2 miles to the south in the town of Guerrero Negro).

Local Attractions
Tours (some on donkeys) to the cave paintings in the Sierra San Francisco. The oldest drawings date from about 100 BC, the youngest from approx. 1300 AD. They are now a UNESCO World Heritage Site.

Information
There is no tourist office in Mulegé. Information on excursions, accommodation, expeditions is available in travel centers. Further information on the official website of Baja California Sur: www.bcs.gob.mx

El Careye's Beach Resorts at the Pazific Coast.

The Loveliest Hotels and Haciendas

Stylish Stays within Historic Walls and Haciendas

Mexico City and the Central Highlands

Habita, Av. Presidente Mazaryk 201, Col. Polanco, 36 rooms.
Tel: 01-55/52 82 31 00, fax: 52 82 31 01,
e-mail: info@hotelhabita.com
From the outside, this futuristic, completely glazed boutique hotel, located in the lively, fashionable quarter of Polanco, looks like an ice cube. Inside, its minimalist design also gives off a somewhat cool aura. But the hotel is "en vogue." Everybody who

is anybody uses the hotel gym for workouts, or visits the aqua spa to recover from the stress of daily life in the metropolis. The elegant restaurant and bar are favorite meeting places for people here on business, or for the grown up children of rich parents who are simply out for a good time: it's an excellent spot for observing the modern, cosmopolitan Mexico.

Casa Vieja, Eugenio Sue 45, Col. Polanco, 10 suites.
Tel: 01-52/52 82 00 67, fax: 52 81 37 80,
e-mail: sales@casavieja.com
The small, luxury hotel is a dream in every respect. It used to be a typical private residence in the chic Polanco quarter, located directly next to the park of the same name. The suites, some of which have two rooms, are appointed with Mexican textiles and furniture and decorated with valuable paintings. Once you've crossed the lavishly verdant threshold, a feeling of peace and tranquillity pervades the atmosphere. No sounds from the big city penetrate into this inner sanctuary. The roof terrace with its bar and restaurant has been set up in a rustic style and decorated with Mexico's most beautiful arts and crafts. The oversized ceramic tree of life is a joy to behold in itself. The elegant Avenida Presidente Mazaryk, with its smart boutiques and excellent restaurants, is within walking distance.

Hotel Nikko, Campos Eliseos No. 204, Col. Polanco.
Tel: 01-55/52 83 87 00, fax: 52 80 35 72,
e-mail: resnkmex@nikko.com.mx

42 floors of cool architecture tower above Chapultepec Park and the Paseo de la Reforma—Mexico City's main thoroughfare. The elegant Campos Eliseos, with more five star hotels, is just around the corner. This classy hotel combines far eastern elegance with Mexican flair. The open-plan lobby and interior shop-lined balconies are decorated with changing displays of art by all that is good and famous in the contemporary Mexican art world. The El Jardín restaurant specializes in Mexican cuisine and serves the best Mexican breakfast buffet in the city. The Teppan Grill, BenKay, and O'Mei restaurants serve excellent Japanese food. The executive floor consists of several levels and has its own bar and restaurant on the 40th floor with a breathtaking view over the city.

La Casona, Durango No. 28, Col. Roma, 29 rooms.
Tel: 01-55/52 86 30 01, fax: 52 11 08 71,
e-mail: lacasona@mexicoboutiquehotels.com
This splendid hotel lies in the vicinity of the chic Condesa quarter, not far from Chapultepec Park and the amusement quarter, Zona Rosa. It is located in a town mansion built at the end of the 19th century during the Porfiriat era. Modern comfort and European-style luxury are hidden behind the façade — itself a protected monument. The floors are not carpeted but have been left as wooden floorboards, accentuating the hotel's historic past. The quarter is home to many other historic buildings and splendid avenues that have been recently restored. There are many nice little cafés, restaurants, and galleries here today.

El Santuario, Valle de Bravo, Estado de México,
Carr. A. Colorines s/n, 64 suites.
Tel/fax: 01-726/262 91 00,
e-mail: info@elsantuario.com
The wellness hotel is located by a huge quartz rock formation on Lake Valle de Bravo over which it has stupendous views. It has been constructed entirely from natural materials in an unusual style. Since its opening in December 2003, it has been regarded as one of the loveliest wellness resorts in Mexico's central highlands. Even sauna guests have a panoramic view. There are 60 different therapies and treatments available.

Mesón de la Sacristía, Puebla, 6 Sur 304, Callejón de los Sapos, 6 rooms and 2 suites.
Tel: 01-222/232 35 53, fax: 232 45 13,
e-mail: sacristía@mesones-sacristía.com
Sleep between antiques, look down over picturesque alleys and watch the carpenters setting their wares out on the street! This cozy hotel that dates back 450 years to the colonial era was once a "vecindad" in the traditional carpenters' quarter — a house in which poor people lived. Today it is an odd little hotel: the lobby is stuffed full of antiques and you can take your pick of the old books that line the high walls in your room, settle down by the window in grandma's rocking chair, and watch the people across the road gossiping. No two rooms are alike and when you come back next time, you'll find that everything has changed: guests can buy whatever takes their fancy and take it home with them. The patio restaurant serves fantastic regional cuisine and if you'd like to take a course in Mexican cooking—sign up right here for one week. A troubadour entertains the evening guests in the unusually furnished Capuchinas bar.

Mesón Sacristía de Capuchinas, Puebla, 9 Oriente No. 16, Antigua Calle de Capuchinas, 7 rooms.
Tel: 01-222/246 60 84, fax: 232 80 88,
e-mail: sacristia@mesones-sacristia.com
This delightful gallery hotel is sister to the Mesón de la Sacristía and matches it on every count of originality and comfort. It is

also situated in Puebla's historic district, just a few walking minutes away from its partner. This building also looks back over more than four centuries of history and breathes an atmosphere redolent of Puebla's colonial times but in contrast to its neighbor's ancestry, the former residents of this house were Spanish colonial masters. The interior and the décor are all antique — and available for purchase.

Quinta Luna, Cholula, Puebla, 3 Sur 702, 3 rooms and 3 suites.
Tel: 01-222/247 89 15, fax:247 89 16,
e-mail: reservaciones@laquintaluna.com
Just a few years ago, this building lay more or less in ruins and goats grazed in the patio. It has been lovingly restored. The small, romantic courtyard now has a bubbling fountain at its center, arcades, and a generous display of geraniums and bougainvilleas in full bloom. The house combines colonial architecture with contemporary designer furniture. There are over 3,000 books in the magnificent library. The hotel is located in a small alley in Cholula, the town next to Puebla, close enough to see the Popocatépetl volcano and the pyramid of Cholula, upon which the pilgrimage church of Nuestra Señora de los Remedios sits majestically.

The South and the Southeast

Casa Tamayo, Cuernavaca, Rufino Tamayo 26, Col. Acapatzingo, 12 rooms.
Tel: 01-777/318 94 77, fax: 312 81 86,
e-mail: lasmusas@casatamayo.com.mx.
The former country house of the Mexican painter Rufino Tamayo is now one of the most beautiful hotels in the "City of Eternal Spring," an oasis of greenery and color situated just a 45 minute drive away from Mexico City. In these rooms, famous artists and writers such as Gabriel García Márquez and Carlos Fuentes, have stretched out to sleep.

Hotel Hacienda Cocoyoc, Cuautla, Morelos, 300 rooms and suites.
Tel: 01-735/356 22 11, fax:356 12 11,
e-mail: hcocoyoc@prodigy.net.mx
The hacienda with the pre-Hispanic name dates back to the 16th century and had seen a lot of history before it became one of Mexico's foremost sugar cane plantations at the end of the 17th century. Situated close to Cuernavaca and Cuautla in the middle of a subtropical paradise, the hacienda was destroyed during the revolution. A private investor purchased the estate in 1957, reconstructed the house and turned it into one of the most beautiful hotels in the region. It has four restaurants, three bars and a disco, three large pools, tennis courts and football pitches. There are two golf courses in the vicinity.

Hacienda Los Laureles, Hidalgo 21, San Felipe Agua, Oaxaca, 24 rooms.
Tel: 01-951/501 53 00, fax: 501 53 01,
e-mail: loslaureles@mexicoboutiquehotels.com
Peter Kaiser, an hotelier of German descent, has been able to realize his very own dream in this restored 19th century hacienda outside Oaxaca. It is situated in spacious gardens with cypress trees and huge mango trees, the rooms are large and elegant. Lectures are held to inform guests about local myths and the pre-Hispanic medical treatments — the benefits of which can subsequently be put to the test in a ritual sauna or Temazcal that cleanses body and soul.

Camino Real Oaxaca, Calle 5 de Mayo 300, 91 rooms.
Tel: 01-951/501 61 00, fax 516 07 32,
e-mail: oax@caminoreal.com
Situated in Oaxaca's historic center on the Corredor Turístico and hidden behind massive walls and a solid wooden portal, the Camino Real is one of southern Mexico's most beautiful hotels. The former Dominican convent enchants guests with its green patios around which corridors and guest rooms are grouped at several levels. The rooms have high ceilings and thick walls. Geraniums, roses, and bougainvilleas flower in the corridors and gardens: orange trees and other ornamental plants accentuate the décor. The wealth of flowers is overwhelming, the pool is huge and set in its own garden. The chapel and the large fountain, in which the nuns used to wash their laundry, are especially eye-catching. Paintings, antiques and ceramics are valuable objets d'art. The restaurant is famous for its varied regional cuisine. Every Saturday evening, a spectacular folklore show (the Guelaguetza) takes place in the former convent church: professional dancers in colorful costumes perform regional dances.

Hacienda San José, km 30 Carr. Tixcobob-Tekanto, Tixcobob, Yucantan, 11 rooms and 4 Maya suites.
Tel: 01-999/910 46 17, fax: 923 79 63,
e-mail: reservations@grupopan.com
Situated less than 30 minutes drive from Mérida close to the sisal-town of Motul, this enchanting 17th century hacienda has been restored with great attention to original detail. The spacious rooms furnished in the romantic-Mexican style and with a ceramic floor are distributed over several buildings in a lush

1 Mesón de la Sacristía in Puebla.
2 Convent garden in the Camino Real Hotel in Oaxaca.
3 Idyllic: the Hacienda Los Laureles in Oaxaca.

combined with onyx, marble and black granite, create an harmonious ensemble of form, line, and unfussy elegance. The huge pool area down on the beach is equipped not only with deckchairs but also with wide mattresses on wooden slats covered with canopies and curtains that guarantee shade and privacy. International chefs such as Michelle Bernstein and Franco Maddalazzo spoil their guests in the various hotel restaurants.

Xalox Resort, Holbox Island; Quitana Roo, Calle Chacchi s/n, Esq. Playa Norte, 9 rooms.
Tel: 01-984/875 21 60, fax: 975 21 60,
e-mail: xaloc@mexicoboutiquehotels.com
A small and sparkling jewel of a resort. The rustic-style hotel run by a young Spanish couple from Barcelona is set on shining white sands in the paradisiacal eco-reserve of Holbox Island, located off the northern tip of the Yucatan peninsular. Getting there takes time — several hours, regardless of whether you are coming from Mérida or Cancun. The last 100 kilometers (62 miles) on a pot-holed, narrow country road that leads to the harbor, seemed to go on and on. But it's worth it. Leave your car on the mainland: the ferry trip is short and once you've landed you'll have to rely on your own two feet or a golf cart — every form of motorized vehicle is off bounds. The fishing village has retained its old-style charm and simplicity. The small hotel consists of spacious, Mayan-style huts designed by the owners themselves and equipped with every kind of comfort. The water glistens turquoise-green, and you can watch the fishermen as they repair their nets and spread their ample catch out on the beach. Each balcony is equipped with hammocks. Watching the sun go down is stunningly kitschy experience.

El Tamarindo Golf Resort, Ciahuatlán, Costa Careyes, Jalisco, km 7.5 Carretera-Melaque-Puerto Vallarta, 29 villas.
Tel: 01-315/351 50 32, fax: 351 50 70,
e-mail: tamarindo@grupoplan.com
The elegant, thatched houses are set in spacious grounds that cover more than 800 ha (3.1 square miles) in a nature reserve on the picturesque Costa Careyes coast, the Mexican-Pacific Riviera. The hotel is synonymous with unsurpassed beauty and luxury. Its clients are members of the internationally wealthy classes and tend towards distinguished understatement. The 18-hole championship golf course is part of the hotel. The wellness center is an oasis within the oasis and the kitchen skills are a revelation

garden. The pool has the unusual feature of having been installed in the hacienda's former water reservoir. The picturesque town of Izamal is close by, home to the largest Franciscan monastery on the American continent. The ruins of an old pyramid are right next door, providing a fantastic platform for views over the monastery, the town and the surrounding countryside.

Ikal del Mar, Playa Xcalacoco, Riviera Maya, Quintana Roo, 29 villas and a presidential villa.
Tel: 01-713/528 78 63, fax: 528 36 97,
e-mail: reservations@ikaldelmar.com
Luxuriant green, virgin jungle; a sea that shimmers in all shades of turquoise and blue and white beaches – this hotel lives up to every cliché ever coined with respect to the Caribbean. Generous, elegantly appointed "Palapas" – huts built in the Mayan style – provide plenty of space. Four-poster-beds guarantee a good night's sleep and hammocks invite you to doze on the terrace during the day – after a dip in the pool. No traffic noise, no petrol stench disturbs this idyll. After nightfall, lanterns light up the paths. The grounds also have a wellness area with traditional Mayan therapies. The cuisine is varied: meals are served in an open restaurant at the pool and in two covered restaurant terraces on the beach.

Maroma Resort & Spa, km 51 Mex 307, Riviera Maya, Quintana Roo, 65 rooms.
Tel: 01-998/872 92 00, fax: 872 82 20,
e-mail: reservations@maromahotel.com
This grounds of this enchanting hotel – a mixture of Mediterranean and Mayan architecture – are situated on one of the Caribbean's most beautiful beaches between Cancun and Playa del Carmen. It is completely secluded, several kilometers off the highway, and exudes calm and intimacy. The Moorish-style baths, the area around the pool, and both the restaurants are particularly attractive.

Fiesta Americana Gran Aqua Cancun, Av. Kukulkán km 12.5, Zona Hotelera, 317 rooms. Tel: 01-52/998 881 76 00, fax: 881 76 01, central reservation office in Europe:
Tel: 0049-69/66 41 96 40 (Frankfurt/Main),
e-mail: resero@fiestaamericana.com.mx
The new Posada-group flagship hotel, opened in December 2004, has already raised the bar for hotel standards in Cancun. Sun, sky and the crystalline Caribbean blue are mirrored in the impressive glass façade. Clear lines and minimalist design,

— created by the icon of "nouvelle cuisine mexicaine" – Patricia Quintana.

El Careyes Beach Resort, Barra de Navidad, Costa Careyes, km 53.5 Barra de Navidad, 29 rooms, 19 suites and 3 bungalows.
Tel: 01-315/351 00 00, fax: 351 01 00,
e-mail: careyes@grupo-plan.com
The El Careyes Beach resort is situated on the curve of a bay with a stunning backdrop — a bit like a Mediterranean village. The rooms and suites are spacious and elegant, dominated by Mexican pastel tones. If bath, shower, huge swimming pool and the sea itself are not enough, try relaxing in your own private pool of rose-petals in the evening — in the comfort of your own room.

Hotelito Desconocido, Puerto Vallarta, Playón de Mismaloya, 12 rooms.
Tel: 01-322/222 25 26, fax: 223 09 23,
e-mail: hotelito@hotelito.com
"The little, unknown Hotel": that's what the name of this unique hotel means. Its palm-covered Jalapas, rustically but elegantly furnished, are situated about 100 kilometers (62 miles) to the south of Puerto Vallarta in a nature reserve with its own lagoon. This is a great place for some undisturbed nature watching, for discovering some of the 150 bird species native to the region — and enjoying incomparable comfort and luxury. It's a paradise far from the beaten track with a unique atmosphere.

Hacienda de San Antonio, Mahakua, Comalá, Colima, 25 suites.
Tel: 01-312/31 34 41, fax: 314 37 27,
e-mail: hacienda@mahakua.com
This elegant colonial mansion used to be the center of a 19th century plantation (for coffee and other crops). Surrounded by an impressive park designed along the lines of a formal English garden, the hacienda is regarded as one of western Mexico's most beautiful country hotels. Features include hand-woven carpets and frescoed walls, paintings by Latin American artists and a large aqueduct made from volcanic stone in the park. The picturesque surroundings and two adjacent volcanoes are ideal for escorted riding and walking excursions. The hacienda has its own large, organically run vegetable and herb garden that supplies the kitchen. Not surprisingly, the cooking here is fantastic.

Quinta Real Huatulco, Oaxaca, Paseo Benito Juárez 2, 28 rooms.
Tel: 01-958/581 04 29, fax: 581 04 29,
e-mail: quintareal@mexicoboutiquehotels.com
The seven bays of the Pacific resort of Huatulco in Oaxaca are the setting for this elegant holiday resort built in a Moorish-Mexican style. Fine woods contrast with polished cement floors and snow white cupolas straight out of 1001 Arabian Nights with palm-covered houses. White is the dominant color on furnishings and lamps of simple elegance.
There is a fantastic view from the so-called infinity pool over the rocky hotel cove. The water is clearer here than elsewhere on the Pacific and the surroundings beckon with paradisiacal, quiet beaches. With a bit of luck, you'll catch glimpses of large sea turtle — and humpback whales in April.

Fairmont Acapulco Princess, Acapulco, Zona Diamante, 1017 rooms.
Tel: 01-744/469 10 00, fax: 469 10 16,
e-mail: aca_reservations@fairmont.com
The luxurious Fairmont Acapulco Princess rises above Revolcadero Bay on the outskirts of Acapulco like a gigantic pyramid that sits enthroned over the smart new hotel district, the Zona Diamante. Built in the 1970s, the elegant hotel has already

achieved legendary status. With its splendid gardens and pool landscapes, its extraordinary wellness area and the different restaurants, bars and discos, including one in the style of a Mayan pyramid — as well as a champion golf course — the Fairmont Acapulco Princess belongs to the top hotels in the world.

3

The Wild North

Las Ventanas al Paraíso, San José del Cabo, km 19.5 Carr. Transpeninsular.
Tel: 01-624/144 28 00, fax: 144 28 01,
e-mail: lasventanas@rosewoodhotels.com
The name of this hotel says it all: "window on paradise." And that's no exaggeration. Each of the 61 rooms — whether with sea or garden view — is a jewel and the service is beyond compare. The butler fulfills every wish. Just a small signal given from the depths of a hammock and he'll be there right away. Raise a small white flag and he'll know that you want to tell him what time to serve lunch. He'll wake you with a small bell — and take you to the restaurant for your heavenly meal. Every waiter addresses you by name. It's just fantastic.

Hacienda de Los Santos, Alamos, Sonora, Calle Molina 8, 25 rooms.
Tel: 01-647/428 02 22, fax: 428 04 67.
The former 17th century hacienda will take you way back in time. The Zapata Bar dates from the revolution (1910–1917) and is a marvelous place to relax.
Open fire-places in each room underscore the romantic atmosphere in this historic house. Only the sounds from the landing strip and hangar for private planes and the four pools serve to remind the guest that we are in the 21st century. The hacienda is a three hour drive to the south of Guaymas in the foothills of the Sierra Madre.

1 Caribbean dream: the Hotel Maroma near Cancun on the Riviera Maya on the Yucatan Peninsular.
2 For VIPs and golfers: the El Tamarindo Golf Resort.
3 Legendary: the Fairmont Acapulco Princess.

Mexican Cuisine

Spicy and aromatic – as diverse as the country itself

Mexican cooking is an attack on the senses – in every sense of the word: so hot that it burns a trail down your throat and then again, mild and aromatic. Whatever its tendency, it is always as exotic and as varied as the country itself. The combination of recipes handed down from pre-Spanish, Aztec, Olmec, and

Mayan eras with Spanish, Arab and French influences make for a unique and revelatory Mexican cuisine.

Mexicans do not see food simply as an act of nourishment, but as a ritual. Restaurants and cafés start the day with tempting breakfast buffets that offer exotic fruits alongside meat and vegetables. Every kind of egg is prepared before the guests' eyes – from scrambled "à la mexicana" with hot chilies, onions and tomatoes or as huevos rancheros, fried eggs on a fried tortilla with hot, spicy red or green tomato sauce. In the north, they add cecina – thinly cut, dried beef. In Yucatan and Chiapas, huevos motuleño – a pyramid of corn, tortillas, fried eggs, peas, hot sauce, cheese and fried bananas – are served. No breakfast is complete without black beans or frijoles, served mostly as a purée with grated goat's cheese.

The Spanish brought wheat, potatoes and other European vegetables to Mexico. But the rest of the world has much more to thank Mexico for in return: the turkey, Tecolote in Nahuatl, and cholocate or chocolatl – not to mention the corn revered by Mexico's indigenous populace, or the leaves of the prickly-pear cactus that are eaten as a salad – and the avocados. The corn mushroom or huitlachoche – also known as Mexican truffles – are a delicacy that is only found here. As are the escamoles, the ants eggs that are a little larger than caviar but smaller than peas and are only available in the spring, when they are served mixed with onions, green chilies, tomatoes, and cilantro. The caterpillars that gives the agaves schnapps known as mezcal (from Oaxaca) that extra kick are roasted with salt, lime juice and hot chilies and served with beer, like potato chips. Roasted caterpillars can be bought by the kilogram on the market in Oaxaca, along with chocolate in every shape and form: with vanilla and cinnamon, or with chili and sugar – a favorite with the Aztecs. Hot chocolate is traditionally prepared with hot water and the use of a specially carved beating device with several rings. Chocolate is also one of the chief ingredients of the Mexican national dish, the spicy mole poblana, a poultry sauce made from innumerable ingredients: different kinds of chili, ground peanuts and almonds, sesame seeds, cinnamon, garlic, tomatoes, onions, cloves, and raisins. The recipe was first cooked by nuns in Puebla who were hiding from government opponents in a convent during the bloody Cristero-War

(1926–1929). Just the smell is enough to make your mouth water. After their late breakfast, Mexicans tend to eat a drawn-out lunch with several courses later in the afternoon. It often starts with a plate of fruit. It's followed by sopa, which generally consists of rice or pasta and is sometimes served with a consommé, or creamed carrots, spinach, broccoli, huitlacoche, mushrooms, or corn. Then, and only then, is the main course – or platillo fuerte – served, with black beans and corn tortillas fresh from the comal – a kind of flat pan. Every table comes with the famous salsas – either in the form of pico de gallo (diced tomatoes, onions, chopped green chilies, and fresh coriander), as a kind of puréed green tomato sauce, or as a sauce made from dried chilies. Any botana (hors d'oeuvre) worth its salt includes the avocado dip known as guacamole served with fried chorizos – the spicy sausages that are part of Mexico's Spanish heritage. Desert takes the form of flan, a caramel custard that is also a Spanish legacy, or milk rice with cinnamon and raisins – and sometimes jellied fruit purée.

Corn tortillas are served in every shape or form: fried in oil as tostadas and spread with bean purée, with chicken or beef, radishes, salad, cheese, cream, and hot sauces; as chalupas with beans and salsa; as taco de pollo, rolled with a chicken filling; as taco al pastor, which is similar to Turkish gyros; or as quesadilla, fried in oil with zucchini blooms, cheese, minced meat, mushrooms, or beans. There's a kiosk on nearly every street corner in Mexico where Indio women sell freshly fried tacos and quesadillas. They are always surrounded, morning, noon, and night, with hungry customers looking for a quick pick-me-up.

The Spanish introduced the wheat tortilla to Mexico. It is of Arab origin and tends to be served in the north as a burrito, fried in the pan with ham, cheese, and jalapeño chilies. Another northern

specialty is barbacoas: fried pork, lamb or goat in freshly baked tortillas served with pork crackling and lots of chili.

The Gulf of Mexico and the Pacific coast are famous for their fish and seafood. Veracruz is known for its huachinango, a kind of sea bass served in a variety of forms but mostly with onions, chilies, tomatoes and olives, as well as for its sopa de mariscos. The famous ceviche, a spicy and very tasty cocktail that consists of seafood or fish marinated in lime juice, comes from the Pacific coast.

The markets are a treat for the eyes: stallholders pile up huge pyramids of oranges, grapefruit, limes, papayas, pineapples, bananas of all sizes, mangos, giant watermelons and red and yellow papayas alongside aromatic guavas. The fruit cocktails and freshly mixed juices are real energy boosters. There are countless kinds of chili on offer: small and fat, long and thin,

Mexican cooking. Tamales, corn meal dough wrapped and steamed in corn husks that are either sweetened or spiced with the addition of chilies, are part of the Aztec legacy – as is chicken or hare wrapped and cooked in banana leaves – and sometimes still cooked in the ground. Everything that is basically edible is used for cooking in Mexico: from beef and pork stomach to marrow, brain, kidneys and heart, even pigs skin and chicken feet! Goats grilled over wood fires are also typical for the north – even the eyes are consumed as a special delicacy. And whilst Germans fight a hangover with marinated herring rolls, Mexicans turn to spicy soups. After a night on the town, they'll make their way to the local market for a huge plate of sopa azteca – a hearty soup made from baked strips of tortilla, avocados, whole chili pasillas, and cheese stewed in a chicken broth – or caldo tlalpeño – a consommé made from pieces of chicken, chick peas, minced onions, fresh coriander and lots of green, chopped chilies. Another classic is the spicy pozole, made from pork and corn.

Mexicans seldom go to bed without a cup of atole, a hot beverage made from corn starch and flavored with chocolate, bananas or vanilla and served with a biscuit. The puff pastries and sweet cakes came over with the Spaniards and continue to testify to the Moorish-Arab influence. The "nouvelle cuisine mexicaine" is a clever combination of Asian, Mexican and European ingredients.

One last thing: chili con carne is not a typical Mexican dish. You won't find this stew, made from black beans and minced meat, on any Mexican menu. It was first cooked by Mexican emigrants and then taken up by Texan cowboys because it is so easy to make: it has now become a staple of the popular Tex-Mex cuisine along with tequila. There are over 250 varieties of this popular drink. Mexican beer enjoys a good reputation – thanks to German immigrants who founded the first breweries in the highlands above Veracruz,

Cheers—and enjoy your culinary trip!

green or red. The long, dark green pods such as the Poblano chili that are similar in form to the Turkish pods, are not quite as spicy. They are considered a regional specialty in central Mexico, where they are served filled with mild cheeses such as the queso oaxaca or queso chihuahua, or with goats cheese, or minced meat, or almonds and raisins.

Dried chilies also abound in every variation. The chili chipotle tastes smoky; the chili pasillo and the chili macho have an aromatic-bitter flavor. Ingredients such as these are guaranteed to turn poultry, venison, beef, pork, and fish into the most delicious of dishes. Herbs such as cilantro, epazote – or wormseed – rosemary, and cumin are permanent features of

1 Wake up drink : freshly pressed orange juice brought to your bed in the Casa Natalia Hotel in San José del Cabo.
2 Tortilla bakery in San Ignacio in Baja California.
3 Breakfast in the Café Todos Santos in Baja California Sur.
4 – 6 Food at its best served in the Hotel Posada El Paraíso in San Cristóbal de las Casas.
7 Taco restaurant in Ciudad Constitución in Baja California.

Index

Imprint

The photographers:

Regula and Christian Heeb, born 1962, are two of the world's most successful travel photographers. Their photos are published in several well-known European magazines and have appeared in over 90 books. They live on a ranch in Bend, Oregon (USA).
Website: *www.heebphoto.com*

The authors:

Susanne Asal studied history, ethnology and English and has been a freelanced travel journalist since 1986. She spent some years in Mexico and Argentinia and is the author of several illustrated books and travel guides. When she is not traveling, she lives in Frankfurt/M., Germany. Susanne Asal is the author of the pages 12-23, 30-39, 76-135.

Herdis Lüke, author and travel journalist, worked in Mexico for 13 years, and subsequently spent many years with dpa in Germany. Today she manages the website *www.mexiko-travelnews.de* and the magazine "Mexiko-Travelnews." She lives in Hamburg, Germany. Herdis Lüke is the author of the pages 24-29, 40-75, 136-189.

Cover photos:

Front: Westin Regina, Los Cabos (large photo); yoga in the Hotel Ceiba del Mar Resort y Spa; butler at the Westin Regina, Los Cabos; Mayan city of Palenque in Chiapas (above, left to right) Front flap: Margarita. Back: Tulum, Mayan citadel, on the Caribbean coast.
p. 1: Nuestra Señora de los Remedios on the temple pyramid of Tepenampa in Cholula in front of the Popocatépetl's summit.

Acknowledgements:

Christian Heeb would like to thank Ana Compean Reyes Spindola of Villa Montana, Frank 'Pancho' F. Shiell in New York, Santiago Canchola, concierge at Villa Montana, Adriana Jiminez in Ciudad de Mexico, Mariana Chavez Montelongo of Tesoros Hotels, Familia Daniel y Teresa Suter-Rodriguez in San Cristóbal de las Casas, Edwina Arnold New York.

Photo credits:

Herdis Lüke, Hamburg: p. 184, 185, 186t.; Fairmont Acapulco Princess, Acapulco, p. 187; Hacienda Los Laureles, San Felipe Agua: p. 185; All others: Christian Heeb.

We are always grateful for suggestions and advice. Please send your comments to:
C.J. Bucher Publishing,
Product Management
Innsbrucker Ring 15
81673 Munich, Germany
E-mail:
editorial@bucher-publishing.com
Website:
www.bucher-publishing.com

Translation: Eve Lucas, Berlin, Germany
Proof-reading: Danko Szabo, Munich, Germany
Design: Werner Poll, Munich, Germany
Cartography: Astrid Fischer-Leitl, Munich, Germany

Product management for the German edition: Joachim Hellmuth
Product management for the English edition: Dr. Birgit Kneip
Production: Bettina Schippel
Repro: Repro Ludwig, Zell am See, Austria
Printed in Italy by Printer Trento

See our full listing of books at
www.bucher-publishing.com

ISBN 978-3-7658-1637-6